# Phoenix from the Ashes

# Books by Suzy Jacobson Cherry

### Poetry
Perfect, Almost

Love in Four Chapbooks

Illusions of Being

Incantations

### Short Stories
Hauntings

Poor Annabella: Vampire (Young Adult)

A Gift for the Princess (Children)

### Spirituality
And She Pondered Them in Her Heart

In Silent Meditation

Mary, Mother of Our Faith, A Short Study

Mothers of My Spirit: Goddesses and Magick

### Memoir
Phoenix from the Ashes

### Divination
Spirit Cards

### No Longer in Print
April Poems

United Methodist History in a Nutshell

# Phoenix from the Ashes

By
Suzy Jacobson Cherry

*10th* *Anniversary Edition*

© 2023 by Suzy Jacobson Cherry
**Tiny Bowl of Cherries Press**

All Rights Reserved

ISBN: 9798860076136

COVER ART ©2008 by Cecilia O'Brien

*Phoenix* is a mixed-media piece created from a photograph of original sculpture by Ms. O'Brien for this book

This book is dedicated to my children, who have made it all worthwhile.

*Once we find the light, we must share our stories to help those who stumble into the dark to find their way. For me, it is important not to think, "why did this happen to me?" but "how can I use what happened to me to make my life and the lives of others better?*

--- Suzy Jacobson Cherry

Take Back the Night Phoenix, 2022

# Contents

Preface to the Anniversary Edition ............................................. 1
Prologue: The Little Girl .............................................................. 3
Interim 1: The Girl in the Corner ............................................. 11
Chapter 1: The Price of Innocence ........................................... 15
Chapter 2: Into Darkness ........................................................... 18
Chapter 3: The Princess ............................................................. 25
Chapter 4: The Fragility of Friendship .................................... 32
Chapter 5: The Risk of Reverie ................................................. 40
Chapter 6: Driving for Dummies .............................................. 46
Chapter 7: Imagination and Education ................................... 50
Chapter 8: The Eye of the Beholder ........................................ 63
Chapter 9: The Ties Unbound .................................................. 68
Interim 2: Back in the Mirror ................................................... 76
Chapter 10: Blood-Rites ............................................................ 77
Chapter 11: Phoenix and the Rock Star .................................. 98
Chapter 12: Rock-n-Roll Reality ............................................ 102
Chapter 13: The Girl in the Song ........................................... 111
Chapter 14: Elf-Witch .............................................................. 120
Interim 3: Through the Glass, Darkly .................................... 130
Chapter 15: Beachmare ............................................................ 132
Interim 4: The Scrying Mirror ................................................ 140
Chapter 16: From the Ashes… ................................................ 142
Interim 5: Dark Moon ............................................................. 153
Chapter 17: Forgiveness ........................................................... 154
Chapter 18: New Life ............................................................... 157
Interim 6: A New Kind of Glass ............................................. 171
Chapter 19: Reunion ................................................................ 173
Statistics* ................................................................................... 178
Resources ................................................................................... 179
Index of Chapters and Poetry ................................................. 185

# Phoenix from the Ashes

# Preface to the Anniversary Edition

I began working on this autobiographical novelette in 1990. In the earliest days of writing, I used a manual typewriter, and I was so angry that I slammed on the keys so hard that they would fly off across the room as I typed. I was angry with my ex-husband as well as with myself. It was difficult to accept the fact that I had been terrible mother, and could not protect my own baby. I didn't think I would ever forgive my first husband. It never occurred to me that I might need counseling. Instead, I entered a two-year period of living two seemingly diametrically opposed lifestyles - careless partying and deep spiritual growth.

Time went by and I tried to begin anew. I had entered a cycle that often happens to those who are still victims of domestic violence, and I was unable to have a healthy relationship. I started a new family twice, both times soon becoming a single mother – first of my two daughters, later adding my son. It was after my son was born that I found myself in a moment of inexplicable forgiveness. Still, it would be many years before I understood how to recognize my "baggage" and put it down before it affected my relationships. In retrospect, I can't help but believe that in that moment of forgiveness, a door was opened to a new reality.

This 10$^{th}$ Anniversary Edition of *Phoenix from the Ashes* has been newly edited and updated, bringing the story full circle. There will be no further editions of this book, though the story may be told in different ways, for sadly the story of violence and survival is likely to continue as long as humanity exists.

# Prologue: The Little Girl

## The Fire

There was once a little girl. When she was small, perhaps six years old, she had a recurring dream in which the house she lived with her family burned down. All that was left was the stove. Snow fell as the little girl and her family huddled about the open stove surrounded by the silence of a cold, dark mid-winter's night. The nightmare was so real, so palpable that one time, the little girl shuffled out of her room, crying.

*"It's just a dream,"* she was told. *"Nothing but a dream; it isn't real. Dreams don't come true."*

Three years later, when the little girl was nine, her family had moved far away from the mid-western city where she was born. They lived in the southwest a while then moved to the west coast. It was here that the dream came true on New Year's Day. Her parents were sleeping late after working at their restaurant jobs the night before. The little girl, being the eldest of four at that time, knew how to cook. It was not unusual in those days for children to be responsible for siblings and learn to perform such household tasks. This morning, this girl endeavored to feed her siblings a hot, steamy bowl of oatmeal.

Since this was in the days before instant cereals, the little girl stirred a cup of grain into a pot of boiling water. Frustrated because she wasn't quite tall enough to reach well, she pulled her baby sister's high chair over to the stove. Clambering into the chair, the girl was satisfied that she could reach well enough to stir the cereal.

She didn't notice until too late that the bottom flounce on her flannel nightgown was close to the flames. All of a sudden, the nightgown was afire, and the terrified little girl began to run around the room, screaming. When it was over, her father had second-degree burns on both hands from putting out the fire. The little girl had second and third-degree burns on sixty percent of her body. Wrapped in a sheet, she rode in the car to the local hospital, where they immersed her in a bathtub filled with ice cubes. A day later, they sent her to the county hospital burn ward.

That first night in "county," the little girl had an out-of-body experience. As she floated above her family's living room, she heard her brother and sisters arguing over a board game. She tried to speak to them, but they didn't know she was there. As she attempted to communicate, a nurse came by her bedside.

"Hush," the nurse whispered. "You're going to wake the other patients. It's only a dream. It isn't real."

Later she was to learn that she had almost died – her parents and doctors were not sure she could make it through those first few days. Her parents came to stay with her for extended periods, pastors and strangers stopped by to visit the little girl. One time, a country singer who was popular with her parents' generation came to see her.

The time in the hospital was an obscure and twisted moment in time when the little girl discovered grisly truths about life outside her small world. For three months her constant companions were hospital staff and fellow burn victims. It was among these others that the little girl found out about the darkness of the human heart.

Her closest friend in the ward was another nine-year-old girl. Her friend had been there when she arrived, and was still there long after the little girl went home. The whispers among the nurses gave the little girl the idea that her friend simply did not want to go home. As it came closer to time to be released from the hospital, her friend would refuse to eat. That's when the little girl learned that her friend's mother had set her on fire.

There was the woman who only spoke Spanish. The large and jovial woman had poured gasoline on herself and set herself on fire. She sat for hours watching cartoons. Her favorite was *Speedy Gonzales*. This woman, too, had been there when the little girl arrived.

Most of the other patients were more transient. Another nine-year-old girl had sat on the steam radiator to see if it was hot. Two babies came into the ward, at separate times. One little boy, a toddler, had stumbled into the oven, which had been left open to heat the apartment, for the family could not afford any other form of heat. The other, a younger baby, was burned on the bottoms of his feet. His grandmother, who was a retired registered nurse, had placed his feet in boiling oil.

No one ever told the little girl the stories that went along with the people in the ward, but she heard them talking. Nine-year-olds are pretty good listeners, especially when they are restricted to beds covered with framework to hold the blankets away from their skin. It was like having her own private tent, where she could hide and eavesdrop on her little world.

The little girl underwent skin graft surgery and physical therapy. After so much time in bed, she had to be taught how to walk again. She was home just in time for her tenth birthday, and finished the fourth grade at home with a tutor. The ordeal was painful and the itch of healing unbearable, but the little girl never really remembered the pain.

She only remembered the fear inspired by the sight of the skin graft stretching and bleeding; and later, the emptiness of rejection when friends refused to hold the hand with the scar.

# Growing Up

The little girl and her family moved around the United States throughout her childhood. Always the new girl, she was rather shy and unsure of herself. When she reached her teens, she dated a little in high school, but only had one steady boyfriend. When she graduated, she decided to join the Air Force.

When she found herself in an environment where there were far more men than women, she found it difficult to discern the difference between someone who might actually have cared for her and someone who saw simply another conquest. Technical school at a stateside Air Force Base introduced her to more than her job.

One night she went to the Airmen's Club with another female airman, where two men they knew joined them and ordered a pitcher of beer. She remembers very little about that night, but it changed her forever. It wasn't until many years later and many weeks of counseling that she realized she had been drugged and raped.

When she went overseas to a base in the South Pacific, she went on a couple of dates with a man who for a bit she thought she cared for, though they didn't commit to one another. During this time, she worked with an older man of higher rank who cornered her daily, pushing her against the wall. He loomed over her and told her she was a woman who needed a man, a real man, like him. She would close her eyes and imagine herself shrinking into the wall. Inevitably he would walk away as if nothing had happened when someone else stepped into the area.

Then one day she accepted an invitation to go out with another man, who asked her to come by his room. It was closer to where they intended to go on their date, he told her. When she arrived, he invited her in to wait while he finished getting ready. When she thought it was time to go and headed to the door, he grabbed her wrist and told her to stay. In the 1980s, researchers would begin using a new term for what happened that night: "date rape."

When she learned she was pregnant, she was unable to know if the father of the child was the man who she thought she had cared for, or the man who took advantage of her gullibility. All she knew was that when she told the former, his response was, "So, what am I supposed to do about it?"

She began dating the man who would become her husband before she realized she was expecting. Though she didn't know him well, she thought she had fallen in love with him after just a few weeks. Not long after he proposed to her, she began to realize that she really wasn't ready to be married. She tried to break up with him. That's when the manipulation first began.

He cried that he truly loved her and that only *he* could take care of her – and the child she was going to bear. He begged her to stay with him. they were married after dating only five months. She was nineteen years old, and had no idea that she was entering a life of fear and loss.

She wanted stay in the Air Force, but when she told the First Sergeant that she was pregnant, he told her she couldn't stay in the service unless she gave the baby up. Soon after he said it, he told her that he and his wife would love to adopt the child. They had raised many children, he said. They would be a loving family for her child. However, knowing this man's wife was stateside while he had a local girlfriend, she refused the offer.

Besides, she wanted her child. So she requested a special discharge from the Air Force and went home to her parents until her new husband finished his tour of duty on the island base. Once he returned, they moved into a small home near the Air Force base where he was next stationed. The verbal abuse began soon after. It wasn't long before what self-esteem she had left after her experiences was gone. A few months later, the physical abuse began.

After the baby was born, he became more controlling and seemed to be incapable of checking his own temper. He began to physically abuse the baby. She was unable to protect her, and prayed unceasingly that God would somehow intervene and save her and the child.

When the baby was five months old, Child Protective Services took the child. The mother was forced to sever her parental rights so the baby could be adopted by a family. The young mother could only hope that the family loved her ever since. It took seven more years before she was able to leave her husband in search of freedom and a new life. Her husband had taken her to his hometown, miles away from her own family and any support she might have had.

Many years later, when she was too old and too busy to re-enlist, she learned that her First Sergeant had misled her about her options with the Air Force.

## Phoenix

She soars free,
trailing gold-red-orange fire behind her
through the blackening sky.
Her beak is made of Dwarvish gold,
Her eyes the burnished scarlet
of lost loves and half-remembered passions.
The feathers, as a fire engulfing Her,
shine golden, crimson, copper -
the colours of sunset and of
dawn.
Yes, She is awesome and lovely and graceful,
this bird from Ancient Lore -
this creature of Light and of Love -
but none save the Faeries, Elves,
Hobbits, and Dwarves
may see this magnificent sight.
No, none save Her fellow creatures of Lore
see this, the midnight flight
of the
Phoenix
this warm summer night.

*©Betsy Jacobson*

# Interim 1: The Girl in the Corner

*I stand before a mirror in a darkened room. Before me are the images of the women I have been in the past. I speak not of past lives reincarnate, but of one lifetime that has been many. Certainly, the faces that peer back at me from the mirror are not my own. Yet, I know that they are. Every one of them is a girl who became the woman I am. Without them, I would not be. That girl, the one cowering in the darkest corner, hiding in the shadows in shame, she is the one who holds me back. She is the one who must rise and declare her part. She must speak, for she has been silent too long.*

*It is important to see her, the girl in the corner. She is too thin. Can you see how her skin has become taut about her frame? Her eyes have sunken in sorrow, smudged with the dark circles caused by worry and loss of sleep. She is skittish; jumps in fear at any slight startling movement. She is quick to leap to the defense of her torturer. She rushes to shush any noise that may cause him distress.*

*The girl in the corner of the mirror does not yet know that she has become a classic victim of a household epidemic. She does not yet know what I know, that she will become free of her captor, only to find herself made alternately more fearful and stronger by the memories.*

*Caught in a cycle of repetition, she will cower in the corner of the mirror, grasping with her bony, anorexic fingers each time I attempt a new life; a new love. Ghoulish, she holds me, as if letting go of me would render her nil. She is as lonely now as she was when I was she. Fearful of nonexistence, she fights the light.*

*I stand before the mirror in the darkened room, gazing at the infant, the toddler, and the little girl that I was. I see the bright rainbows of childhood become dark cloudy spots as the teen years begin, when the comfort of family is no longer enough and the first rejections shadow the young girl's fragile soul.*

*I see the bright sunshine of first love and the introduction of magic awakening the spirit of the burgeoning young woman. Then: there she is. First love rent asunder and torn from the arms of parental protection by virtue of "growing up," she has forgotten the rainbows. Now, she only knows the shadow. I see it in her eyes*

*I stand before the mirror in a darkened room, and today, I reach for her. Through the glass, through the boundaries of time, I reach. Perhaps if I can touch her, she my anti-matter, we shall be destroyed and a new me come into being.*

*Perhaps I will become the woman I should be. After the explosion, perhaps I will stand proud, and strong, and capable. Perhaps I will stride forth without fear into a meaningful, truthful, and loving life. Perhaps I will become the Phoenix, rising from the ashes.*

# Chapter 1: The Price of Innocence

When Phoenix reached puberty, her mother told her about sex. When Phoenix, trying to understand the Ten Commandments, asked, "What's adultery?" her mother knew that it was time. She told Phoenix the difference between "adultery" and "fornication," and that when an adult man and woman fell in love, they got married and then they had sex. It wasn't just about love, her mother told her. It was about marriage and responsibility as well.

So, when Phoenix was seventeen and fell in love, she wouldn't have sex with him because he wasn't ready to marry her. She knew it had been a true love, for her belovéd stayed by her and honored her wish to remain virgin. She knew then and she knows now that he had respected her.

The two were more than boyfriend and girlfriend. Phoenix had begun to explore spiritualities outside the current of mainline Protestantism in which she had been raised. He was a student of esoteric religion, and in the early days of their courtships, he had become her mentor. Phoenix felt a sense of connection to him that she thought spanned the boundaries of time and space. She hung her teenage dreams on his knowledge and his love.

She thought that when she was ready, she would one day say yes to his gentle advances. In her mind, the first time she had sex would be a magical experience, tender and memorable.

However, it was the 1970s, and her love was a little bit older and a little bit freer in his lifestyle than she was. It wasn't enough for Phoenix that he loved her and honored her – she expected him to cut his hair, hold a job, marry her, and find her a piece of land with a house and a white picket fence. His hippie-sense of freedom and desire to help her "expand her mind" were frightening to Phoenix, and to her parents. In spite of loving him and knowing her loved her, she asked him to move on.

### Clean Heart

I washed my heart
With the love of others
Since I asked you to go
When will it come clean
Of you?
Or, will it ever be so?

© *1976*

Two years later, Phoenix was pregnant by another man and engaged to wed another. After high school, she joined the Air Force. With no intent to marry and the dream of perhaps one day getting an education and becoming an officer, she went from Basic Training to technical school with stars in her eyes and her patriotism on her shoulders. She put up no protective walls against the dangers present in an environment so long commandeered by men and the "good ole' boys."

After a brief and somewhat confusing "girl crush" on a female British Flight Lieutenant who commanded the women at Basic Training and dreams of becoming "just like her," Phoenix slipped far too easily into the tantalizing grip of a young man who resided on the male Airmen's floor in the student dormitory. He played the part of the suave New York Italian flirt; he called her a pet name that hearkened from a favorite situation comedy, and Phoenix fell for it like the innocent she truly was.

One night at the Airmen's Club, having a drink with another female student airman, Phoenix felt joy when the debonair "gentleman" and another man joined them. One of the men bought a pitcher of beer and the last thing Phoenix remembered from that night was walking out the door intending to go back to the dormitory. Flashes of memory bounce in and out like a strobe light:

*He offers her a ride back to the dorm; she resists, he insists.*

*She's standing in front of a hotel front desk.*

*She's waking up in a hotel bed naked, hurting in places where she's never felt hurt before.*

*She's bleeding and there's blood all over the bedsheets.*

*She wants to go back to base alone, but has no idea how she would get there.*

*He comes into the room talking as if nothing had happened.*

*She has no memory of the night before beyond the small bright flashes.*

*She feels empty but for a deep sense of shame and embarrassment, which will remain for years to come.*

From that day until she left Tech School, he avoided her and she reddened from shame any time she caught sight of him. Random female Airmen came up to her, whispering unkind things they said he told them about her. She had no idea what she had done to deserve such treatment. Not knowing what to do, she shrank into the woodwork and focused on her training.

## Chapter 2: Into Darkness

Once Phoenix graduated from Technical School, she flew 9,000 miles away from her home and family to the tiny island of Guam. In her emotional immaturity, she was too young to understand the dynamics of young men and women confined together so far away from home, in a place with a ratio of eight men to one woman. She had not realized she had been raped in Tech School, she only knew that the once-imagined "first time" was not a magical experience, but a black hole in her memory.

Certainly, Phoenix did not recognize that she was being sexually harassed when the large, twenty-or-thirty-something fellow cornered her, forcibly kissed her, and insisted that she didn't need a *boy*, she needed a *man*. Nor did she recognize date rape when she went out with the nice-looking young man who insisted that her timid "no," was really a flirtation – after all, she *was* attracted to him…wasn't she?

In her naiveté, Phoenix somehow convinced herself that these were honest attempts to gain her *affection*. Most certainly, Phoenix did not understand her own emotions and desires. Inside, she was a ball of tangled thoughts, fears, and intermittent emptiness. In some ways, although she consciously believed she still had hopes and dreams for her life, Phoenix had given up. Having lost the opportunity to give herself in love to someone who appreciated her, she began to find herself thinking she was in love whenever a man paid her any attention. Believing this, she gave them what they wanted, thinking that in this way she would find emotional fulfillment.

She would never forget the moment when she met the man who would become her abuser. They worked together in the dining hall kitchen. When their eyes met the first time, Phoenix felt her knees weaken. He was a somewhat sullen young man with a thatch of thick mahogany hair and deep blue eyes. His almost translucent, ivory skin was peppered with light brown freckles that gave him a look of boyish innocence.

Phoenix was taken in by the illusion and believed herself to be utterly in love.

There is a grain of truth in an old saying Phoenix had once heard that "good girls get pregnant – bad girls know what to do about it." Phoenix had not considered birth control, for she had never intended to give herself to any man until much later. By the time she was nineteen, she was a child about to bear another child, and the man she was marrying was insecure, manipulative, and soon would show a violent side she never suspected.

Phoenix had barely begun to discover herself when the destruction commenced. She was gullible for a girl growing up in the 1970s. She had no experience with the domineering sort of person to whom she had bound herself. Coming from a loving, close-knit family, a person like her fiancé was simply not in Phoenix's frame of reference. Her innocence and insecurity lowered what resistance she might have had. At first, Phoenix did not see herself as submissive. After a while the problem was that she did not see herself at all.

They had been married for a few months by the time he first hit her. He had said something to her, and when he didn't like the response she gave, he pulled back his fist and slammed it into her chest. The fury of it took Phoenix by surprise. Not until many years later would she realize that she should have seen it coming.

In retrospect, Phoenix found that if she tried, she could see the whole thing unfold before her like a bad fairy tale. In the months before that initial physical manifestation of his hatred, her husband had begun to wear down any strength she might have had. It started before the wedding, when she began to feel inexplicable trepidation about the potential of being married to him. He cried, literally begging her to stay with him. He professed his love and declared he would not be able to go on without her.

He had coerced her into leaving the Air Force once they married. His desire for her to discharge from the service was reinforced by their First Sergeant, who told Phoenix that she could not be in the Air Force and also keep the child she had recently discovered she was carrying. She had not been around long enough to carry the diamond edges of experience; she thought he honestly did it out of love.

After the marriage, the verbal abuse began, and thus began Phoenix's death of self. She began like shale, and the layers were easy to break away. She was a slut, he said. After all, he reasoned, she had slept with someone else before him. The proof was in the oven, so to speak. No matter that she had remained a virgin until the age of nineteen, in the midst of a sexual revolution. No matter that she had no choice on the night she lost her virginity, after so many teenage dates saying no to boys with wandering hands.

Worse yet, according to him, Phoenix was a "*stupid* slut who couldn't do anything right." Everyone knows that his way (or his mother's way, or his grandmother's way) is the only correct way of doing anything. Phoenix didn't know how to hang clothing on the line properly, she folded the clean clothes incorrectly. She couldn't do *anything* right.

Phoenix had been taught to cook at an early age. Soon, however, with his expert assistance, she was rendered helpless in the kitchen. It wasn't long before all she could do was burn fish sticks. For some reason, she found it difficult to watch over the cooking meal while dropping everything to run to the living room when called to change the television channel or to refill a glass when the ice was shaken like a servant's bell by the man who sat in his rocking chair waiting for her response.

As a man, he ascertained, it was his right to sit in leisure while his wife ran circles around the apartment trying to keep up. The food burned. The meal ended up against the wall or in Phoenix's face as he wailed to the universe:

*Why did he ever get stuck with such an ignorant bitch, anyway?*

## Submission vs. Dominance

Always
Someone dominates;
Someone submits
There are no equal relationships
One leads – one follows
One cries – one consoles
Fair? I cannot judge,
But only comment
On what I see
Is this Eternity?

© *7 July 1977*

Phoenix began to believe what he told her. He repeated it so often that it was second nature for her to know beforehand that she was bound to do it wrong, so why try? She did not realize that she had changed so much. She could not see what she had become, so when he actually hit her, Phoenix was shocked.

When it happened, she threw herself on the bed and cried. After what seemed like hours, he eventually came in and told her how sorry he was. He fervently promised that he would never do it again. She truly believed him that first time. She tried to believe it over and over again, each time his fist or steeled toed boots made contact with her flesh.

**Identity Crisis**

All muddled
Befuddled
She sits by the glass
Looks in at
Herself; looks back
Not her, no not her
Is she there, or even,
Is she?
He twists it, he kills it
She's gone.
But look:
She flits by –
A flame in the heart:
Now it dies.
A nice word, thick with
Love
Is cut short by a snap.
She is dead.

© *4 June 1980*

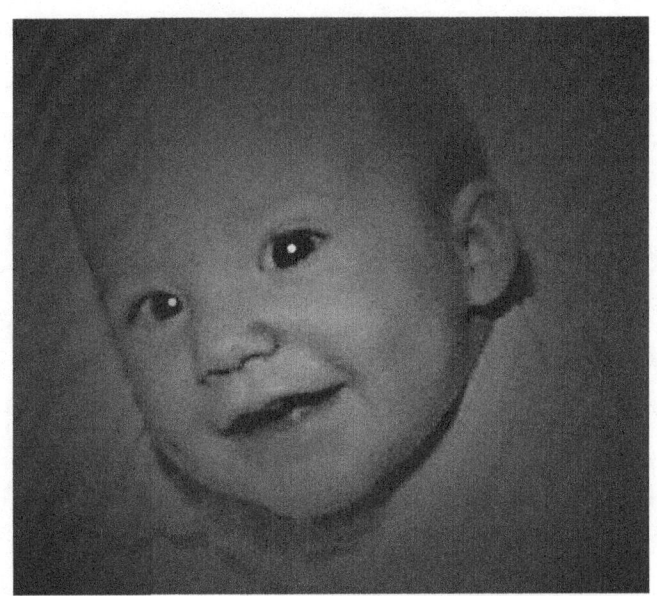
*The Beautiful Princess*

## Chapter 3: The Princess

Phoenix was still alive when her daughter was born. She was barely hanging on, but she could still breathe…a little. Her daughter was a beautiful child, a perfect child. All the right parts were in all the right places, and her big brown eyes smiled up at her Mama with all the trusting innocence and sweetness in the universe. How could she know that the loving arms that reached out to welcome her into the world could never be a haven? How could she know that the one person who should have given up life for her was already dying herself? For a little while, the two of them were full of each other, and the world seemed to be a happy place. Phoenix called her special child Princess.

Princess however, being royal and therefore very delicate, was colicky. Colicky babies cry. Phoenix held her baby close. She rocked her, fed her, and comforted her. She did all that she knew how to do, but it was never enough. So, after a few sleepless nights, *he* decided to take the problem into his own hands. After all, he knew how to shut up his mouthy wife, didn't he?

From that point on, Phoenix could no longer be the protection that the little Princess rightly expected from her mother. People who have never been in her position will always ask why she didn't just take the baby and run. She could have gone home to her mother and father. Phoenix's parents had always been the sheltering arms that parents should be. If she had garnered the courage to leave, her family would have supported her. At the time, though, it was impossible for Phoenix to make such a bold decision.

Only those who have been there have any comprehension of the various factors that cause a woman to remain in an abusive relationship. These factors worked together in Phoenix and murdered the maternal instinct that would have caused her to flee. Psychologically, Phoenix had been manipulated into believing that she deserved everything she got, and when she didn't hand over that squalling brat immediately, she would get it again, and worse than last time.

The first few times, Phoenix fought back viciously, and received a pummeling as payment. She feared for her life and for the life of her child. But when he said, don't worry, I promise not to hurt her anymore, some little part of Phoenix wanted so badly to believe it that she almost *did* believe it.

There is a fear of failure that can work like quicksand. Stuck in the pit of despair, the victim fights to no avail, finding that not only does fighting not save them, but it pulls them further into the mire. Phoenix was in the middle of the pit. She thought that if she did not keep trying to make her marriage work, trying to do better, then there was one more thing that she could not do right. Innocence can be blinder than love, and she had made a vow that bound her. Phoenix's belief in the sanctity of one's word was as old fashioned as mint juleps on a southern verandah in the afternoon. After all, there was that vow: "For Better, For Worse."

Those four little words have for centuries thrust unsuspecting and trusting women – and not a few men - into hell. If you just wait long enough, Phoenix would think, better has *got* to come. And she was a martyr for it. All the while she was being martyred, she prayed – fervently but silently – that somehow her little Princess would be saved. She couldn't do it herself; she was too weak, too fearful, and too ashamed to admit, even to herself, that she was what she was – a victim of abuse.

Since Phoenix was unable to shelter her Princess, someone else had to. Friends called in the authorities. It was not long before Phoenix's arms were empty, and some other woman held Princess, loved her, and changed both her diapers and her name. To this very day, Phoenix does not know exactly how it happened. She does not know why her own parents could not take the Princess. They believe that she said they could not have her; though she remembers distinctly the social worker telling her that Princess could not remain in the family. In retrospect, Phoenix wonders if *he* may have coerced Phoenix to disallow options that she would have preferred. She does remember, however, asking the social worker if she left him, could she get her daughter back? No, the social worker told her. It would not matter.

That was the day that Phoenix gave up and gave in to what seemed to be her fate. What purpose was there fighting? No one offered her any choice of options; such as, if she left him, received counseling, and got a job, she could one day get her Princess back. They did not give her any option; they did not offer her a counselor. The authorities did not see her as someone who needed rescuing, and so they left her there, lost and empty. Why fight? There was nothing to fight for.

In retrospect, Phoenix cannot help but wonder why she could not regain custody of her Princess, had she left him, gotten counseling, and engaged the support of her family. Was there some other family who really wanted the baby? Did the social worker lie to her? Perhaps it was best that she did not get her back; perhaps it was best for the child. Thankful that she was at the very least somewhat recognized as a victim rather than a perpetrator, Phoenix always believed that wherever her baby was, she was given a better life than Phoenix could have given her. Not to believe so would be too much to handle.

*He* got counseling, though. He was hospitalized. He was tested. He was medicated. The psychiatrists said he was sick. He was very sick, so he hurt her and he hurt her baby, but he told her he loved her and that he needed her. He insisted that his illness meant he needed her more now than ever. How could she even think of leaving him?

After his diagnosis, he reminded her often that he was sick and needed someone to love him and care for him. When he wasn't "guilting" Phoenix into staying, he was threatening. He swore vehemently, and convincingly, that if she left him, he would find her and he would kill her. If he couldn't find her, he swore, then he'd just deal with her family – one by one. It's no wonder Phoenix stayed with him.

Phoenix has few coherent memories of this time in her life. Foremost in her mind are her disappointment in the social service organization that ignored *her* cries for help and gave her daughter into the arms of a stranger, and the fear induced by a vicious man who had once seemed so tender.

There is still the confusion that remained much later when her parents voiced their feeling that she should have turned to them for help. They could not understand that she couldn't come to them when she should have. Only she knows that by the time this happened, she had become so rooted in the fear and the dark of her husband's twisted mind that she could not escape. Like a maiden wandering in a maze in the recesses of a medieval dungeon, Phoenix was lost in the abuse. She was not able to escape into the light to reveal her wounds.

Deep inside, she wonders if they had seen her bruises, so deftly covered by makeup and lame excuses. Deep inside, she wonders if things would have been different had they had the power to physically remove her from his possessive grasp, though reality assures her that they could not have done so. Deep inside, she still feels the emptiness left in a heart violently rent asunder by the theft of her one little light of hope.

There will always be a space in the middle of Phoenix's heart where the infant Princess once resided. Most often it is covered by a thin layer of scar tissue, grown by the passing of years and her love for the children who came much later.

Still, the emptiness is a constant darkness for Phoenix, the only variable being the intensity of the feeling. The passage of time may lighten the load, but it cannot completely obliterate the sensations of guilt and sorrow. Many days may pass when there is no thought at all of this terrible loss, but sometimes the memory is awakened.

### Sanctuary?

Hole in my heart
You are a missing person
I gave you away
You never asked
To be taken from my love
You never cried
To be kept within my Haven.
But then, I never
Gave you Haven.
Hole in my heart,
You will never be filled
It is with sorrow
I leave you open
There is nothing
To place
In the space
Where you were
© *4 January 1983*

Birthdays can be the worst time for anyone who has lost a loved one. For Phoenix, birthdays would bring up the loneliness and the sadness. It rekindled the great guilt that she bears in not being a safe place for her infant. On birthdays, Phoenix says a little prayer for the child she didn't raise. She asks only that the child was raised in a family where she could have the safety Phoenix was not able to provide.

Truly, time, no matter how long it may be, does not erase the emotions of love, loneliness, and guilt. A wounded heart never fully mends. Guilt remains to darken the pit of the stomach, to bind the solar plexus with a black mass of molasses-thick sadness. Oh, yes, the light may shine for a moment or for a year, but then comes another birthday.

**Birthdays in January**

Birthdays in January
Are bleak, speak
Of barren forests
Open to the raging
Fires of destruction.
Long ago winters
Writhing in snow
Pushing forth spring-times
Destined to fail
Groundhog,
Why didn't you tell me
Cold winter was
Bound to return?
Birthdays in January
Are dark
The promises
Of a sweet, yawning spring
Are yet too far away
© *4 January 1983*

**Eleven**

Yesterday was your birthday
Almost a woman now, and I
Never knew your girlhood
I miss you so
Did you remember, when you
First cried, "Mama"
That there was another, long ago?
When you learned to walk,
Did you scrape your knees?
Did your teeth make you cry?
Did your new Mama hold you?
I wasn't there when you
Went off to school
When you first learned to read
When you got your first crush
I'll never know if you
Cried in the night
Or got in a fight
Or have brothers and sisters who
Love you.
I gave you life
I gave you my heart
But I never could give you safety
I'm sorry for the sadness
For the pain
For the fear
I'm sorry I never could help you
Forgive me one day?
Always I'll pray
And keep this empty place
In my soul

© *8 January 1989*

# Chapter 4: The Fragility of Friendship

Once the Princess was gone, Phoenix's situation steadily worsened. Her husband had more psychiatric evaluations and was discharged from the military with a disability. His illness had a name, they said. According to the paperwork, his illness was "schizophrenia, undifferentiated type, with paranoid tendencies and delusions of grandeur." Armed now with a bottle of Thorazine and a legitimate excuse for dropping out of real life, he took to his rocking chair.

Giving him a name for his problem and leaving him in a marriage with an un-counseled partner was rather like giving a hunter a rifle and license to kill in the local deer park. It seemed to Phoenix that he took to his rocking chair solely to devise new ways of tormenting her, as well as schemes of earning a living vicariously through her. It was paradoxical: he constantly told her that she was incapable of doing anything right around the house, yet he expected her to function in the world of work and bring her paycheck home to him.

They had offered her counseling, to be sure. She attended one session before he refused to allow her to go. Since Phoenix didn't drive, he would have to take her to her meetings and pick her up. During the ride home after the first session, he coerced her to tell him everything the counselor asked and every answer she provided. She had not opened up to the counselor that day, though any small bit of truth she may have shared would have earned her further punishment from her husband.

After his discharge from the Air Force, he took her back east to his hometown. The small mill city was thousands of miles from anyone Phoenix could call family. At his goading, Phoenix corroborated his story that their precious little baby had died of Sudden Infant Death Syndrome. Though this story was accepted by all who heard it, the lie was too much for Phoenix's fragile conscience.

One night at a party consisting of the only friends Phoenix was allowed to have – his friends and family – Phoenix confided in her sister-in-law. Phoenix believed that women would stick together in such a situation. The sister-in-law promised faithfully not to say anything to her husband – or anyone. Phoenix has no doubt that the sister-in-law truly meant it when she made the promise. Unfortunately, neither woman had taken human nature and self-preservation into account.

Though Phoenix's brother-in-law was barely thirty years old, the sister-in-law in whom Phoenix had confided was his fifth wife. Phoenix's brother-in-law was an extremely violent man. When he became angry, he beat the woman he professed to love with studded belts and threw her into the tub, turning the shower on with scalding hot water. He had even once nailed the bathroom door shut after beating her and throwing her inside. Phoenix and her husband often got together with his brother and his wife to play cards. They been present many times when his brother lost his temper. After she told her sister-in-law what had actually happened with her little Princess, Phoenix realized she should have known not to share the story.

Her brother-in-law was so violent that when she was present during one of their fights, Phoenix always wanted to cry out, "Stop, leave her alone!" or at least, to run and hide herself, but she could not. Her husband would stare her down with a look that said, see what happens when you don't watch your mouth? See what happens to a woman who contradicts her man? If Phoenix happened to find some nerve and open her mouth to speak during such events, her husband would place his hand on her shoulder and squeeze while whispering these very words into her ear.

The episodes between her brother-in-law and his wife were so terrifying that it came to pass that Phoenix actually felt *fortunate* that her husband did not wear studded belts. At least he never tied her up and tossed her into a steaming hot shower.

Strangely, however, this same man always treated Phoenix with respect and tenderness. It was as if, not having her as his own, he could appreciate her as her own husband could not.

One day a month or so after Phoenix had confided in her, the sister-in-law thought she was pregnant. She decided that perhaps it would be best if she left her husband, for she was terrified. Knowing what she did about Phoenix and the little Princess, she knew it would likely be worse for her, for she knew her husband was the worst of the two brothers. If things had worked out the way the sister-in-law planned, she would have been long gone before her husband found she had left. However, for some reason he returned home early that day to find his wife packing up her personal items. Confronted, the sister-in-law broke down. In her fear, she told him that she was pregnant, and that she had to leave. In support of her decision, she inadvertently blurted out Phoenix's story. The truth is, of course, brothers often *do* stick together. His brother told her husband what Phoenix had told his wife.

Phoenix was working the first shift at a plastics factory at that time. Like the wire mill where Phoenix and her husband had worked together previously, the factory was within walking distance from their fifth-floor walk-up near the river. The walk home took Phoenix past City Hall and through the small downtown shopping area on the High Street. She recalls that it was a gorgeous day, the kind of day when the sky is a certain blue that brightens moods and inspires hope. It was the kind of day where the few clouds in the sky puff whispers of secret laughter as if angels had gathered for tea and gossip. As she walked home that day, her heart soared hopeful, momentarily forgetful of the danger that lurked behind the front door at the top of the stairs, the door to the place that she called home.

Carefree, she came to a crosswalk. It was there that the hopeful came to an abrupt end. Looking across the street, Phoenix saw her husband waiting for her on the corner. His livid face loomed largely before her like a sudden close-up in a horror film, and her heart sank. She knew in the pit of her stomach that she had done something wrong. Fighting the urge to run, Phoenix crossed the road to where he waited, and walked full-on into his fist. He virtually dragged her home by the hair that day. In the manner of a comic Cro-Magnon, he held her blonde locks tight and pulled until they reached their fifth-floor apartment almost six blocks away.

Perhaps that was the first time he banged her head against the wall so many times and so hard that she knew it really was possible to see stars. How many times had she seen this in cartoons and thought it was just a joke? As he slammed her head against the kitchen wall, he cried accusations at her. She was untrustworthy. She was unfaithful. She was being *purposefully* mean to have told the true story of the Princess to his brother's wife. He cried that he felt guilty about what he did to the baby, how bad he felt, and how terribly, terribly cruel she was to subject him to this torment by talking about it to someone else. At the time, Phoenix was abjectly sorry, and forgave him his anger. She knew she had betrayed him. After all, as he had reminded her so very often, it wasn't his fault. His mental illness had made him do it.

Mental illness or not, the results of his behavior had affected Phoenix deeply. She had come to the point that she had lost her own identity. What had she become? Was she a person? Did she have the right to her own thoughts, her own friends, or even her own life? She had never been allowed to deal with her grief. Phoenix learned never to speak of it to anyone again. The shame she suffered at the loss of her life was immeasurable.

Looking back on those days, Phoenix often wonders if his mental illness was diagnosed correctly. The medications he was given were unpleasant. They caused him to sleep too long and to suffer sunburn if he went out for too long during the day. Eventually, he refused to take them. Could things have been different if medications were more advanced? Might his diagnosis have been more precise, if he had been diagnosed twenty years later?

## Brand

Don't stare;
She is not blind
The blue beneath her
Eyes is but the
Stain of her affection
There is nothing
Upon her face except
The mark of her
Transgression
(So he told her, so she believes)
Funny, she thinks —
How before, she could do no wrong
How now, she can do no right
What really hurts is that
It is with love that she
Receives the blows
(And no one ever
Told her before, that
That's the way love feels)
Optimistically, she looks to the future
Prayerfully,
She tends to the scars
Of this inequity
But nothing, not even the tears,
Will wash them away

*© 13 October 1982*

Since those days, Phoenix has known many folks who have lived with various mental illnesses. She discovered that an uncle she had remembered as somewhat strange had suffered from severe depression and undergone electroshock therapy in the 1950s. Family members with diagnoses of bi-polar and severe anxiety disorder have made her aware of a need for improved treatment for these conditions. However, at the time of her first marriage, Phoenix had not knowingly experienced life with a person with mental and emotional disorders previously. All she knew was that he was ill, and she hoped he would get better. In retrospect, she knows she should have mustered all the courage she could and walked away, for her own emotional and mental health.

Instead, she tried to trick herself into believing that she lived in a loving home, with the kind of husband a young girl dreams about. When she was away from home, she conjured pictures of a cozy, warm home where the husband was willing to pay the cost of heating the entire apartment and the wife did not have to curl over the top of the gas-and-gas stove with a hot cup of tea to warm her fingers while she read a book. She imagined an autumn when she could lounge on the couch, feet up, with her tea beside her, soft music in the background while she read, cats curled at her feet and a loving husband who came by to kiss her "just because."

Reality was a stark contrast to her imaginary home, though she tried to make it a place of welcome and love. She added small touches of hominess when she could. She cleaned house diligently. She brought lovely bits of nature inside. Lilacs and curling ferns created a space where it was easier to feign happiness, though it be momentary. She made feeble attempts at levity now and again, hoping laughter could truly be "the best medicine."

## October's Cold, Hard Pavements

I sit upon the steps/cold pavement
Chill sets in; October dampness
Death may; Nay it MUST
Feel much like this:
Marrow stiff as ice
Rigor mortis, setting in,
Impedes my movement
THEN: A thought; upstairs
Awaits eternal warmth
And little feline souls
Celestially sing requests
To curl upon my lap/live blankets
Up there; sweet music,
Hot tea, good books await
And there, amongst
My furry friends,
Dwells One whose Love
Is cherished far above the others
I MOVE: October's death has not yet
Squelched my wisdom
I turn, negotiating
Stairwells dark from autumn
Warmth radiates above;
Love permeates my soul
No longer shall I lose myself outside
Upon October's cold, hard pavements

*© 10 October 1983*

## Chapter 5: The Risk of Reverie

Phoenix's life at that time was not always so bad. There were brief moments of contentment. When she was home alone, she would often lose herself in music, a book, or poetry. In these moments, she felt like herself. She loved those times when she could put an album on the stereo, brew a hot cup of tea, and curl up on the sofa with a good fantasy story. She could almost forget the prison within which she dwelt.

There was even some semblance of happiness when she and her husband took long weekend drives into the New England countryside. They would drive for many miles, stopping at yard sales and antique stores, searching for something to make him happy. Phoenix was always glad when he found something – an old postcard, a vintage magazine, or an ancient camera would thrill him.

Momentarily, he would seem kind. In the car, when he wasn't speaking to her, she could gaze out over the scenery and pretend she was a wandering outcaste in some nonexistent renaissance. During these times, she would send herself to some plane of existence where she could walk alone in the forests of Merrie Olde England or Scotland, with no man to guide her hand or keep her down. Perhaps she would be a witch or an herb woman – perhaps a friend to the faerie folk.

In some of Phoenix's fantasies, she fell in love. Always, her dream-lovers were nothing like the man she strove to erase from her mind. The dream-lovers were always tall and blond, like her first love, and when they said they loved her, they meant it. They had kind and gentle hands, their lips were soft, yet passionate. The dream-lovers were not afraid of the intimacy of love, neither physical nor spiritual. They came into Phoenix's imaginary forests with a great passion for life and a wondrous sense of adventure.

**Methinks**

How the Renaissance river
Cools my tired feet
I've been walking for days
On this rugged terrain
(It's the gipsy in me – methinks)
I come slowly from Glasgow –
Must leave the dirty, grimy city
This fresh dewy green is healthy
(I've ne'er a horse to my name)
I can see that the matrons of the country homes
Disapprove of a young girl
Like me, travelling alone
I can take care of myself
(It's the Viking in me – methinks)
I sing softly a ballad
Of the Good Queen Mary
And then:
I eat a cherished loaf
I'd had to bargain well to get it
(It's the Scotsman in me – methinks)
On I forge:
Through forests of trees and beasts,
And I know
I will conquer the world
I have become free,
And I'm winning –
All power, all wisdom,
And Queen
(It's the Saxon in me – methinks)

© *1983*

## Chamber Music

Lying lazily beside a brook
I hear a poet softly singing a love song
Accompanied gracefully, quietly
By the strumming of his lute
Chamber Music.
I am sitting now, with my slippers by my side
I dangle my feet in the water and weave a daisy chain
To wear in my hair but no one else is there
In the distance, where there is a road,
I can hear a gipsy wagon clattering noisily –
Tambourines and laughter
I am young, and I wonder – will I become old, and how?
Footsteps rustle behind me
Swirling the fallen forest leaves, and I turn
It is the poet, his lute in hand.
He smiles gently, "Dear Lady,"
He says, a song even as he speaks
"Dear Lady, sing with me."
And I do. Chamber Music.
Love Songs.
He takes me by the hand, And I ask,
"Where do we go? You are a minstrel, a traveling poet.
Tomorrow you shall be gone to sing to the Queen."
He stops a moment, and touches my cheek
"You come with me, Sweet Lady; together we will charm the
Hearts of the aristocracy."
So, together we travel –
Together, we show the Lords and the Ladies that love
Is enough
Two poor minstrels, happily in love
Traveling, playing,
And singing Love Songs.
Chamber Music.

© *1981*

Most of the time, Phoenix had a strange sense that she was not a genuine person, but that she was like a plastic doll, forced to act by some invisible and malicious being. Yet, often after one of these reveries, she would begin to feel as if she had somehow become real. She would begin to open from a dark cocoon that she had built around herself. When that occurred, a little light of Phoenix's own personality would shine through, and she would forget herself.

She would share a thought. She would voice an opinion. Perhaps it would touch upon a crucial subject, such as the meaning of life, or of love, or even of what she would like to prepare for dinner. Most often, though, the matter would be insignificant. Usually, it would be a matter of Phoenix's emotions; a matter of the heart.

For instance, there was the time when he was teaching her how to fly fish. Phoenix had never done such a thing before – nor had she the inclination. It was her preference, when he went fishing, to spend time sitting with a book on a rock near the river, enjoying the warm breeze. She would sit in the dappled shade drinking iced tea, dipping a toe in the river, while enjoying a good fantasy story.

This day, however, he decided she would like to learn how to fish. It had been a beautiful New England summer day. The grass was green, the water clear, and the trees and brush in full foliage. Phoenix had been reasonably at peace when they began the drive into the countryside, but now she was having some difficulty with her wrist action. Unable to understand how anyone could find the wondrous art of fly-fishing so challenging, her husband became more frustrated by the minute. It was not long before he engaged in a tirade.

After fifteen or twenty minutes with him screaming into her face that she was an idiot, Phoenix found it difficult to even hold on to the pole. Her hands trembling, she bit her lip and struggled to hold back the tears. Eventually, he decided that it was foolish to think he could teach such an imbecile the cryptic secrets of fly fishing. She was good as a tackle carrier, no more. He gave up.

As they packed the car with the untouched picnic supplies, fishing tackle, and rods and reels, he poured upon her such a tirade of verbal vomit that fear overpowered her. She mumbled something to herself, perhaps, "why?" Having heard her small voice for a moment, his avalanche began anew. WHAT DID YOU SAY? IF YOU'RE GOING TO SAY SOMETHING, SAY IT OUT LOUD, CALL ME NAMES TO MY FACE!

Phoenix always found it hard to discuss anything rationally during the onslaught of abuse. She could barely cause her voice to react with a lump in her throat that felt the size of a golf ball. She tried to swallow it, to open her mouth, to defend herself. She could not. She said nothing. Once the automobile was loaded and they were on the road toward home, she made an attempt. She swallowed hard and choked back a tear.

"When you yell at me," She said, "I get scared and I can't do anything right." The man was incredulous. *I scare you? How do I scare you? If only you weren't so stupid, I would have more patience with you!*

"But," Phoenix said, swallowing the golf ball by sheer force. "But –." No other word was able to free itself from her throat. For "But" is one word too many.

His balled-up backhand whopped into the side of her face and the sting brought a fountain of saltwater to her eyes. "Don't!" She cried, and he spat, SHUT UP BITCH! DON'T YOU EVER KNOW WHEN TO SHUT UP? He hammered the back of his fist, barely taking his eyes off the road. When he tired of hitting her – or perhaps his knuckles just began to hurt – he pulled the car to the side of the road and bodily dragged Phoenix by the hair from the vehicle.

He kicked her once or twice with his karate-trained steel-toed boots, and hopped back into the car, leaving Phoenix standing sobbing on a highway fifty miles from nowhere. Afterward, she thought she should have hidden somewhere for a time, and later hitchhiked to somewhere, anywhere else- or at least, home to the mid-west. However, she was too afraid to make such a courageous choice. "For better or worse" echoed shallowly in her mind. Could it get any worse? Soon he returned to pick her up and take her home.

### A Band of Gold

Who ever thought a band of gold
Could tear so much apart
Instead of building loving arms
It's a chain upon the heart
A little thin; that golden ring
A tiny piece of stone
Ties two together now as one
And never left alone
A bar across life's window
A wall around the mind
A little think' who'd ever think
It a magnet of that kind
A band of gold, inscribed with love
Turned friendship into fear
A band of gold; inscribed with love
Turned friendship into fear
A band of gold, a little vow
Killed love that once was dear

*© 9 August 1985*

## Chapter 6: Driving for Dummies

Phoenix did not learn to drive a car as a teen. Like most kids, she had gotten her learning permit and had one lesson in a parking lot with her patient father as a teacher. However, soon after her first lesson, the family moved to another state and Phoenix began her senior year of high school.

There was never time that year for her to learn. Soon after graduation, Phoenix joined the Air Force, where she found that there was no need for her to drive. There were buses on base that went into whatever town happened to be close by. After her marriage, her husband dropped the notion here and there that it was doubtful that she would be capable of commandeering such a dangerous machine on a public highway. Certainly, he surmised, she would never attain *his* level of expertise.

After all, she sometimes thought with secret sarcasm, he was actually able to maintain a steady safe highway speed while driving a standard four-on-the-floor and pummeling the girl he "loved and cherished 'til death do us part". She couldn't even grovel, beg for mercy, and cook a decent dinner simultaneously. Even so, in spite of his obvious desire to keep Phoenix tied to his tethers, he decided he would try to teach her to drive whether she wanted to learn from him or not.

His teaching technique involved the belief that the best way to learn anything is by total immersion. After driving her to a town ten miles away from home, he told her to drive the Volkswagen Beetle home. It seemed to Phoenix that he timed it carefully, guaranteeing that at a certain point, she would be forced to concentrate on both the clutch *and* rush-hour traffic while anticipating his anger. His frustration was bound to fester, for her terror was evident and she seemed unable to keep from grinding the clutch. It was not long before Phoenix had to add the interference of large hot tears running down her cheeks and the wrench of her hair wrapped around his hand as he pulled it out to her concentration effort.

When he finally had her pull over so he could shove her to the side and take over the driving himself, Phoenix was a puddle of dark goo, unable to sense any sort of emotion. She didn't even care that he drove straight to his grandmother's house to tell the woman what an idiot he was married to. Phoenix, with her red, puffy balloon-face and two-inch eggs growing on the side of her head, sat in the car.

He took his time visiting with his grandmother. She was a kind woman, who had raised this man and his siblings after their parents divorced. Phoenix always liked visiting her, for she was always offered a nice cup of tea and conversation. Sometimes, his grandmother would teach Phoenix how to make some of her favorite recipes, though during the marriage, Phoenix never once took the risk of making one of them for her husband. By then, she was fully aware that her efforts could never match that of his grandmother.

While she waited, as she had so many times, Phoenix let her mind begin to wander. She entered her internal alternate world, where she felt safe, calm, and prepared. Her fantasies whispered once more through visions of green and long-time-ago romance. This time was different, though. This time, she found herself envisioning a new direction for her life. This time, the route to safety seemed so simple, so direct. So quiet…so soft…so welcoming. Death seemed to be her only friend, inviting her to join him in the world beyond the veil.

## The Willow

Lying beneath a willow tree
I know the willow –
The willow knows me
Together we weep;
Together we cry
Sobbing so gently
(The river flows by)
There's nothing so sweet
As a great weeping willow
And soft grass below
To use as a pillow
Sleep will come quickly
My tears will soon dry
Then: into the river
To my tree, a goodbye

© *1981*

# Chapter 7: Imagination and Education

After so many years of being called names that she herself would never have spoken in those days, Phoenix was beginning to doubt her existence as a real person. The numbness in her heart was pierced only by periodic physical pain. It was pain inflicted by the hammer hole in her knee, steel toed combat boots indenting her shin, or a screwdriver tossed mumblety-peg into her thigh. These were the small scars left to remind her of her descent into invisibility to this very day.

It's amazing how such injuries can return later as the body ages. Slipped disks and arthritic fingers bent early remind Phoenix of the days when she was that other girl, the one who had become invisible. The days when she was the girl who only knew that she was alive because of the pain. Death would have released her from the fall into a cold nothingness. Somehow, though, the invisible Phoenix remembered deep within herself that at one time, she had been a real person. She had once loved and grown in a normal fashion.

Amid the days and nights of his throwing everything messy in the kitchen all over the stove and table, then kicking her into it, slamming those steel-toed boots into her back while spitting on her as she attempted to clean it up, she remembered herself. The memory was buried very deep like a treasure lost in a time long before. The only things that kept Phoenix near sanity were her words, her books, her love of learning, and the memory of her first true love. In the end, it was the combination of all these factors which saved her from the tormenter her husband had become.

One day, Phoenix dared to write a short story about a girl. The main character was someone much like herself; a girl who was lost, a girl who was invisible. As she wrote, she was careful not to make the life of the girl in the story too much like herself. She feared that if her husband found it, he would punish her for revealing too much about their secret life. She named her character "Agatha." Agatha's life was nothing and everything like the life Phoenix endured. Writing it down in a spiral notebook in longhand was both heart-wrenching and cathartic. When the story was done, Phoenix hid it away.

## Agatha Reborn

*Agatha is sitting, once again, looking out over the city street. She is shrinking. It is a slow process, this shrinking. Slow – but unalterable. As she sits silently by her window, Agatha remembers a time when she held herself in full form – straight and proud – a time when a future loomed large and bright before her. She had dreams of fame, of poetry published and remembered. In those days, Agatha had been much like Mary, sister of Martha and Lazarus, a woman given to books and to learning. She had been certain that her path would follow the intellectual. But this day, sitting lonely, Agatha has come to realize that she has stopped growing. She sits back in her rocking chair, gazing with empty eyes at the dirty city two stories down, and sees herself. She is shrinking, smaller and smaller. Soon, she will be an infinitesimal dot, small and black. Soon she will shrink into nothingness.*

*She has been sitting here a long while. The housework is done in but an hour. , the baby sleeps away most of the day. What else is there to do, but sit? She looks at the clock. It's four-thirty, time to start dinner. Frank will be home soon, and dinner must be ready. If he comes home to an empty table, there will be hell to pay. There is no excuse, no reason acceptable. Agatha winces as she stands and gingerly rubs yesterday's bruises. "Dear Jesus," she thinks, "What was it I said this time?" and then she shrugs. No use to wonder – it isn't worth the pain. She trusts that the answer will come when it's supposed to. As she prepares a casserole, Agatha's thoughts flit about, wandering, lighting here and there and speeding past the painful things, searching for a pleasant spot to land. Suddenly, she realized that it was on* her wedding day that the shrinking had begun, "Why is that?" she wonders, "Where did it start?"

Before she was married, she remembers that there had been a whole self within. Original thoughts had seeded in her mind, growing often into full ideas and expansive dreams. It has been only in the last two years that she has faded. Two years that seemed an eternity. That continuous, imprisoning, shrinking had reduced her mind to its minimum long ago. Now, her thoughts and words were simply redundant of something her husband has said, or something he needs or wants.

Frank's key rattles the lock, jarring Agatha back to the present. She wipes her hand on her apron, and limps to the door whispering a prayer that tonight go well, that she may have time to heal. The limp is only slight, this time. Thank God, this night's battle was mild. She has been through worse.

"Hi, Honey!" she greets him cheerily. He grunts a hello and stiffly kisses her on the cheek. It is a robot-kiss, planted impotently on her face each evening. "When do I eat?" His voice is tired, bored, and a little gruff. Agatha quickly becomes the image of efficiency. Any passerby, able to see in the kitchen window, would see an American housewife, aproned and smiling, scooting about the kitchen. She is June Cleaver in blue jeans, Harriet Nelson in a ponytail. As she finishes preparing the meal, sets the table, and pours the milk, Agatha wonders how she can possibly reach. She is so very small now.

"Come and get it!" she calls. Is it her imagination, or is her voice becoming smaller, too?

They eat together quietly, making small talk. Frank talks droningly on about his work day. Agatha has heard it before and can no longer hear him as she lets her minute mind search for its resting place. She thinks she loves him. For some reason unknown, she thinks maybe he loves her.

*Frank is a good provider, a hard worker, and sometimes can be very loving. When it is his desire, his eyes become soft, his words tender, and his touch gentle. Agatha is attractive, caring, and obedient. Everything Frank ever wanted in a wife. He especially admires an obedient woman, and he was careful to "break his wife in" as soon as she was his. He considers her well trained, and boasts to his friends that he knows just how to keep his woman in line. He boasts, too, that Agatha wants his kind of love, for isn't she still with him, giving him what he needs — a maid, a mother, a listener, and a lover?*

*Looking into Frank's eyes, Agatha wonders if it will matter to him if she fades completely away. Will he notice? His voice drones on, something about a co-worker, but Agatha cannot hear him. It just doesn't matter. There had been a time, she thinks, when they had been intellectually equal. Once, before their wedding, there had been two-way conversations. Now, she can do no more than parrot him. They have become one, and it is his personality which prevails. Sometimes, Agatha has to stop and force herself to remember her own name. She thinks that maybe if she had kept her maiden name, she would have continued to exist. Maybe if she had left him the first time he hit her, she would still be a person.*

*These thoughts whirl through Agatha's head, but she realizes that they are but fantasies created by her idle mind. Leaving has never been a possibility for Agatha. She is a strong believer in keeping vows, and she has stuck by Frank "for better or for worse," always praying that the worse would bet better. Before the wedding, Frank had worshiped Agatha. In those days Agatha could do no wrong in Frank's eyes. Now, she can do no right. Every time she attempts anything, she makes a mistake. She doesn't make her bread the way his mother does, so she is wrong. She isn't as strong as his sisters were, so she is incapable. It must be her fault, she thinks. It's all because she's shrinking. When you shrink, you lose your capacity to function correctly. It is her failing, not his. There is no reason to leave. It hasn't yet occurred to Agatha that Frank's expectations of her have caused her to shrink. It is the proverbial vicious circle, and the guilt continues to bear down upon her, crushing her into the tiny, faded being that she is becoming.*

*Now that supper is over and Frank is stationed before the television set, Agatha bustles about the kitchen. She is careful not to disturb his concentration as she washes dishes and sweeps the floor.*

*"Why don't you come sit by me a minute?" he calls in. Agatha laughs. There is still so much to do. "Well, at least come and change the channel for me, and bring a beer when you come!" At this, Agatha frowns, and pulls open the refrigerator.*

*The baby is beginning to whimper. Agatha rushes to the crib. He must be picked up before he has a chance to bother Frank. Frank has seemed angrier since his son was born. Agatha sighs. She had always believed the stories of fathers and sons going fishing and to ball games; daddies bouncing babies on their knees. As she lifts her son from his crib, her injuries from the night before shoot pain through her like razor blades, and she gasps.*

*Moving to the rocking chair, Agatha sits, holding her son close. As he nurses, he looks into his mother's eyes. He searches her face with that look of knowledge particular to infants, as though he remembers some other place and time that he had loved this woman. Sometimes it seems to Agatha that this child could see her very deepest thought, and she was ashamed that there should be so little left for him to find. As she sits nursing him, Agatha sinks once more into meditation.*

*A baby had not been in her immediate plans before she met Frank. It was to have been college and a career in journalism or teaching. She wanted children, desperately, but not until she was no longer a child herself. But then, love, lust, or some insidious infatuation had broken her dream. "Why am I shrinking?" she wants to scream into the baby's face. "Where am I going?" instead, she hums a lullaby. They sit quietly in the growing purple dusk that has fallen across the baby's room.*

*Silently, thoughtfully, she places the sleeping baby in his crib. A thin smile begins to emerge as Agatha remembers a pad and pencil kept, for some forgotten reason, here in the nursery. Taking them in hand, she sits back into the rocker and scratches out an idea which as suddenly seeded itself in her barren mind:*

> The bruises
> Are not so much
> For the pain
> As for the decoration
> She is his,
> No doubt about it
> But give him
> Another chance — she will

*Agatha has written a poem! It is the first in over two years! The shrinking of Agatha's being has suddenly shrieked to a halt. She places the pad and pencil deep below a stack of diapers and leans over the crib to kiss her son. As she leaves the room, she stands at the door, looking back at the place of her rebirth. It will be in this room now, beside her sleeping son that Agatha will begin to grow anew. She rubs away a single tear, softly closes the door on the womb of her fetal soul, and returns to the prison she will escape when she is born.*

© *1983*

As she wrote, Phoenix decided it was time to submit some of her poetry for publication. The local newspaper had a column that did that sort of thing, and after a time, Phoenix became a regular contributor. It wasn't long before she won a poetry contest. With the prize money came temporary understanding and acceptance from her husband. He gave her permission to begin reading in public, at festival gatherings.

For a time, he seemed to support her, though he never attended a reading. If he had, there is no doubt he would have relished the introductions when it was his wife's turn to read. For, only he and she were aware of the terror he instilled on a daily basis. The poems Phoenix shared at readings were idyllic fantasies. No one would ever suspect the ravaged soul that she had become. In her effort to escape reality, Phoenix was able to project a persona of pure confection. Misled by Phoenix's stories of illusory anachronistic dream lives, the host of the poetry events introduced her as an innocent. Ironically, the poem that won a cash prize was written about the loss of her little Princess.

**Glaciers**

I have tried, tried
Tried to pour out warmth
But I live on the edge
Of an Ice Age

I have cried, cried
Cried to sing out love
But the tears have
All frozen to glaciers

No small smiles
Will melt the frozen land
For I live
On the edge of an Ice Age

© *1983*

Having found a new doorway to the world, Phoenix began to recall what it meant to be a real person and to be happy. While her husband did not encourage her ventures into the big world of the arts, for a moment it seemed as if he wanted to see her happy. In reality, he had gone back to school himself using his GI Bill, so he had his mind on other things. As long as Phoenix kept herself in line with his expectation of a wife and homemaker, brought home the income, and wrote his college papers for him, she had his permission to play "poetess."

The papers Phoenix wrote for his classes earned him A's and B's though she never attended a class in Art History nor studied *Hamlet*'s Soliloquy. It was a fair tradeoff, in her estimation. Get him good grades in his academics, keep him in school, and hone her craft all in one activity. This idyllic situation was short-lived. The day came that he asked her what she expected to do with this writing "thing." Did she think she was going to be a female Ernest Hemingway or something? It was a nice hobby, he said, but nobody really wanted to read girl's poetry. He assured her that she was wasting her time.

His cutting remarks could never stop Phoenix from writing, publishing, or reading at open mics. She had, in fact, been writing since the age of 12 and had even been published before she met him. She did, however, realize that he was not going to support her in an attempt to focus on writing as a career move. Phoenix had now been married to this man for many years. She had learned to survive by devise, and now she found a way to talk him into letting her join the National Guard so that she could return to school. The state they lived in provided free education at state colleges and universities for National Guard members.

Phoenix made him see that should she have a better education she might be able to make more money. He had made her use her own GI Bill grant to attain an Associate in Science in Medical Secretarial Science, because he had heard that Medical Secretaries demanded high salaries. Of course, once she had graduated and found work in the field, she found that his information was not exactly correct.

Phoenix had earned her degree while working full-time because her husband was unable to work due to his mental illness. Now it seemed time to continue her upward educational trend. He let her begin. Sitting back in his rocking chair, he rubbed his hands together, contemplating riches. She went back to the community college at night, continuing to work full time.

Once she attained her second Associate Degree in Liberal Arts and Science, Phoenix got a part-time job and began what was to be her first semester at a major university. She was a National Guardsman now, so she spent one weekend away from him.

Ironically, the Guard took her away from her educational pursuits once more. When a full-time secretarial position with the National Guard became available, she had no choice but to accept it. Her husband had lost his vision of an enriched future before Phoenix completed her first semester at the university. Once that semester was over, so was her educational career. She began to imagine that one day she would re-enlist in the Air Force. Of course, when she brought up the possibility, her husband's reaction ended that daydream.

Phoenix kept writing. Writing is something that is in the blood, and she found ways to use it in her job. As she expanded from school papers and short poems into local military regulations, Phoenix began to write more short stories as well. Her first short stories were extensions of her daydreams about her first love. She found herself imagining what it would be like to find him, to be with him again, perhaps forever.

Although Phoenix knew in her heart that there was a good reason why they were not together, the imaginings of a bigger-than-life romance became subject matter for stories and poems. The fantasy that created the stories and poems kept

Phoenix from curling up and swallowing a bottle of anything that would just make her fall asleep and never wake up. Writing made Phoenix feel visible.

Writing reminded her that she was an entity unto herself, in spite of the fact that her husband had directed almost every action and decision of her life for so long. The one area of her life that he could not control was her imagination. The stories brought that imagination into reality. A sophomore level university course called "Major British Writers" introduced Phoenix to the Romantics. The Brontë sisters, particularly Charlotte, led Phoenix to new ways of giving her imagination life through words.

### Catharine's Dark Night

Dear Heathcliff:
They cannot understand
Thy soul (My soul)
They: who are not *we*
Find evil in your being
No, they cannot see
You are what they made you
Our love is forever, our Soul is one
Come to me, Heathcliff
In the darkness of the night
Your Catherine cries…sighs, soon to die
Yearning for your Soul's
Encompassing love
Come to me, Heathcliff
In my wicked despair
For soon I shall
Wander alone amongst
The rugged crags of
Wuthering Heights
Searching for your
Ever-grasping arms

© *24 August 1983*

Phoenix associated the romantic tales of yesteryear with the story she held in her heart about the man she had once loved, whom she had sent away. Her memories of him were colored by her deep need for escape from the life she lived today. It was a life that seemed little different from the lives of those characters who were buffeted about by the whims of a ruling class and the mores of a harsh patriarchal society.

Memories and dreams of the man Phoenix had loved as a teenager awakened her yearnings for something better. When her first two-week summer training for the National Guard came along, Phoenix realized that something better was possible. Strangely, it was through one of her greatest fears that she learned that she was strong and capable.

Phoenix was terrified of heights. It was, perhaps, her most tangible fear. During her training, she had the opportunity to overcome that fear — twice. Her position as Administrative Technician for the Law Enforcement Unit allowed her the chance to complete the obstacle course challenge along with the Law Enforcement and Security Police airmen. At the end of the course, looming largely before her stood the wall. It was sixty feet of angled wood, built for rappelling practice.

Since Phoenix was not a police person, completion of the rappelling exercise was optional. Somehow, though, to Phoenix it became imperative that she make the jump. It took all the fortitude she could muster to climb to the top of the wall. After being rigged into a harness and assured that the airman acting as "safety" at the bottom knew his job, she walked to the edge of the wall, turned around backwards, and dropped. Her heart fell into her stomach and she gasped for air.

Suddenly, she was upside down, dangling from the top of the wall. There was a momentary flash of terror as she swooped around, hanging head first, feet in the air. After a moment's hesitation, she recalled the instructions that had been given before the group started gearing up. She had hesitated, letting fear overtake her as she fell backwards, so her bottom stuck out, throwing off her balance. Now she righted herself, and used her feet to keep herself from slamming against the wall as she slid down the rope. Success!

Phoenix, the woman who had been diminished almost to nothingness; the woman who, according to her husband, was incapable of making even the slightest decision on her own, met her greatest fear in battle and had won! Heartened and determined to do it without the error of ending up upside down, Phoenix climbed the wall once more and completed the exercise a second time. Oh, yes, she made mistakes on her way down; nevertheless, Phoenix stood at the top of that wall and dropped backwards, trusting, into the abyss.

### Rappelling

Perched high,
A lump in my throat
And rope
Strung gently through
My hands
I sigh, and backwards
Drop to empty freedom
One above and one below
I know, though
Fear has filled my inner being, that
Without this I could never know
The strength in trusting others, nor
The freedom found
In having
Neither foot upon
The ground

© *19 July 1985*

For years, Phoenix would think of this as the time she truly overcame her fears. Though she would do many brave things throughout her life, this was her most significant measure of courage, for she believed that it was the one that anyone could understand. Surely nobody else could comprehend the courage it took for a secretary to pick up the telephone to make a simple phone call, for an adult student to stand before a classroom full of young people to give a speech, or for a battered woman to walk away from the man who made her life into a truly living hell. But facing a true bout of acrophobia, people could understand that.

## Chapter 8: The Eye of the Beholder

So many years of being told that no one else would ever be interested in her had ingrained in Phoenix an utter belief in her inadequacies. She truly believed that she was stupid, ugly, and fat. Phoenix weighed no more than 110 pounds by this time. During the course of her marriage, she became bulimic because he had insisted that she was getting fat. Phoenix stood five foot three, was medium boned, and her ideal weight in her twenties would have been somewhere around 125 pounds. Even with that, when an old girlfriend of her husband's referred to Phoenix sarcastically as "fat," Phoenix took it literally and was ashamed.

She had been proud walking with her husband one spring day, wearing hip-huggers and a halter-top. It was an outfit she had dreamed of wearing, but she had always been self-conscious about baring her tummy. As a teen, when she wore the popular halter tops, she walked with both arms folded across her belly, hiding what she perceived to be fat. This day, as the two walked along a street just a few blocks away from their apartment, they ran into an old girlfriend that he had never mentioned before. Once he made introductions, the old girlfriend snidely remarked, "Oh, you're really fat, aren't you?" He laughed and Phoenix stiffened at the unbelievable rudeness.

They never saw the woman again, and Phoenix never wore the hip-huggers and halter-top again. She lost a few more pounds. Convinced more than ever that she was becoming grossly obese, she starved, exercised, and vomited herself to a tiny 105 pounds. It wasn't until many years later that Phoenix realized that the woman was probably being facetious.

Once Phoenix began writing, meeting new people, and attending school, her bulimia began to correct itself. She still ate very little, fearing to eat more than an apple or an orange unless she was bingeing with her husband in front of the television. She did stop vomiting, however. Her obsession with exercise continued into her new Air National Guard career. The constant attempt at losing more weight was simply a physical extension of the psychological invisibility from which Phoenix suffered.

With the physical conditioning requirements in the Guard, Phoenix found a network of support for her fitness obsession. She put on weight in muscle and began to fill out her clothing once more. Working on the base full-time allowed Phoenix to add fitness video workouts, three-mile lunchtime runs, and alternating five or six-mile bike rides at lunch to her regimen. It was no longer simply a survival technique: for Phoenix; fitness had become a lifestyle. She still felt ugly and obese, however. After all, her husband never neglected to point out how fat she was.

It was on a National Guard trip to the Air Force Base at Myrtle Beach in South Carolina that Phoenix learned that there were men who found her attractive and intelligent. It may have been the next step in rediscovering herself. As Phoenix was the Administrative Technician in her unit, she spent most of her training time helping in the Personnel Office of the active Air Force Base. She didn't enjoy it.

Once she had completed the Law Enforcement obstacle course with her co-workers, and gained the loving title of "Rambette: the Secretary with the camouflage typewriter," mere office work seemed tedious. However, her hours were regular and much shorter than those of the rest of her unit. Because of this, Phoenix was able to walk alone to the beach in the afternoon.

Walking through the base, she had time for reflection. The weather was lovely and the walk served her need for solitude. When Phoenix reached the beach and took off her overdress to lie on a towel in her bathing suit, she noticed the men nearby on the beach looking upon her with what she perceived as admiration. She doubted her interpretation, but the sensation was pleasant and she felt as though perhaps her husband was wrong when he told her she was too ugly for anyone but him to want to be with her. When she went out "on the town" in the evenings with some of her co-workers, her heart soared at the sound of live music and the dance beat of the discotheques. Men asked her to dance, bought her drinks, and attempted to seduce her home with them. None of them slipped something into her drink.

This was almost an entirely new sensation for her. As a teen, she had been shy and reserved, believing that only one man – that early love of her life – found her desirable. When Phoenix joined the Air Force just out of high school, she was caught up in the party attitude of the Airmen's Club, pitchers of Sloe-Gin Fizz or beer with her classmates and girlfriends, and dancing all night. She felt popular and beautiful back then, until that fateful night. Before she had a chance to get used to feeling good about herself and incorporate a level of maturity into her extracurricular life, she was broken. Soon after, she was to Guam where she experienced another sexual assault and sexual harassment. She met her husband, and it all ended abruptly. Now, her trips to the beach and into town made Phoenix a tiny bit bolder. A small flame of passion ignited in her spirit.

At Myrtle Beach, she found a friend in a young Security Policeman on the base, a gentle soul with a sweet Virginia drawl. She would sit with him at night at the guard shack as he checked the identification of those who entered the base. She found another friend in a young rock-n-roll singer with long, wavy chestnut hair. She talked with them for hours, telling them things she had not been able to speak aloud to anyone else in all the years of her marriage.

She even wrote song lyrics to share with the singer in hopes that one day he might find a way to put music to them. It was probably not a good song, but in her head, it rocked; a story of the proverbial casting couch and a woman much like Phoenix wished she could be.

### Woman of Principle

I could have taken her far
I could have made her a star
But she didn't like the way it made her feel
I could have made her a name
But she wouldn't play the game
Said no way she'd ever make that kind of deal
She was a woman of principle
A woman of strong hard will
A woman of principle
So I wouldn't let her stay
Funny how I love her anyway
I could have put her name in lights
If she had given me her nights
I told her everybody did the same
But she had it in her mind
That she wouldn't be that kind
And she wasn't gonna lay her way to fame
She was a woman of principle
A woman of strong hard will
A woman of principle
So I wouldn't let her stay
Funny how I love her anyway
She was a woman of principle
A woman of strong hard will
A woman of principle
So I wouldn't let her stay
Funny how I love her anyway

*© 15 July 1985*

Neither of these young men would be likely to remember the sad and sallow blonde they met that summer, but Phoenix will never forget them. In her heart, they will always be good friends. It was because of her friendship with them that Phoenix gathered the strength to make the decision she was soon to make.

### Pebbles

My friend: and still
I care for what you think
And wonder what you think of me
Time passes, and your face
As it was before
Ebbs in and out
My mind like sand
Beneath the crashing waves
Lonely pebbles rolling
One by One
Stopping close, then caught by
Foaming tide and once again
Float off
Alone

© *19 July 1985*

## Chapter 9: The Ties Unbound

Just over a month after Phoenix returned from her National Guard training, she left her husband for good. It was not an easy thing to do. Her fear of retribution was ingrained and intense. Once she made the decision, she made a long-distance call to her family. It was the only way she knew that she would follow through. She knew that if she told them she was leaving, there would be no going back on her decision. Her maternal grandmother purchased her plane ticket, arranging for it to be waiting at an airport two hours away.

There was an entire week's waiting period before her Monday flight, and Phoenix knew inherently that if she slipped up in any way, he would find out, and she might not survive the aftermath. She sought strength from within, for she knew the only way she could survive the week was through sheer willpower and an inexplicable calmness of soul. Phoenix had the irrational sense that her husband would know of her plans telepathically, so she carefully guarded even her thoughts.

### The Origins of Peace

And peace,
A royal offering – long lost among
The jewels of state,
For brothers hate.
Oh, pray, sisters,
--Everywhere—
This birthright's
All you seek – You are not weak
Oh, sister, search your
Bountiful heart,
Your secret soul –
It's hidden there –
Come, won't you share?

*©13 April 1984*

Since Phoenix still didn't drive, she carpooled to work with another airman. During that last week, she smuggled as many small things that mattered to her as possible out of the apartment. She stacked them into her co-worker's Corvette when he picked her up in the morning. As she stashed the boxes and bags in her office, she offered no real explanation of what she was doing to anyone. It's a trite observation, but for Phoenix, it was the longest week of her life. Every day that week, Phoenix worked hard at behaving normally, fearful that her husband would find out that she was leaving.

On Friday, Phoenix had to take a great risk, for it was necessary that she resign from her position and request a transfer from her National Guard position. The Base Commander called her to his office, to ask her if there was any way they could persuade her to stay. It was the first time that Phoenix verbalized her intuitive knowledge that if she remained in the same geographical area, her husband would exact retribution from her for leaving him.

It was difficult to admit to the Colonel that she had nearly been living a double life for eight long years. She was forced to describe some of the treatment she had received at her husband's hands. When she finished, the Commander accepted her resignation, signed the necessary papers, and gave permission for another co-worker to drive Phoenix to the airport on Monday.

Now that she had spoken it out loud, Phoenix's fear intensified. She had the irrational fear that somehow her intentions would manifest themselves in her behavior or that her husband would suddenly become psychic. She virtually held her breath throughout the weekend. Her husband knew someone from the base, who could easily have picked up the telephone and told him that his wife was planning to leave.

The base recruiter was her husband's Judo instructor. After hearing what she was up to, he came to her and told her he thought she should tell her husband of her plans. This person had no idea the intensity of her husband's anger. She managed to talk the Judo instructor into keeping her decision to himself, at least until she was gone.

The weekend seemed to take forever to pass. When Monday morning arrived, she verged on hyperventilation until her co-worker dropped her off at the airport. Even then, it was tenuous, for she had yet to pick up the ticket and wait the long two hours until she had boarded and the plane reached cruising altitude. She sat at the edge of her seat with the boarding pass clutched tightly in her hand. She was terrified of losing it. Her eyes darted back and forth, watching every man as if he might suddenly transform into her nightmare.

Eventually, they called for boarding on her plane. She jumped up and rushed to the gate. When she finally allowed herself to breathe, it was with a sigh of relief that she had held in for eight years. She pondered the fact that she was heading now to a cold place, and fleetingly wished that her parents had stayed in the southwest, where they had lived when she was younger. Of places she had lived throughout her life, the desert seemed the most welcoming and warm. In spite of not having been to the desert southwest since she was a young child, she remembered her friends and the teachers who had inspired her.

She had fond memories of playing with her siblings and friends in the desert behind their small apartment complex when she was in third grade. She thought now of the walk through a small riparian area on the way to a small store where they would purchase penny-candy and gum. She recalled a moment in time when she stood beneath a cottonwood tree, watching tiny "angels" swirling from the branches, caught in the wind and carried across the small wash where dragonflies flitted to-and-fro.

Now she sighed and lay her head on a pillow provided by a flight attendant. Closing her eyes, she shifted into a dream.

### Salt of My Tears

Why aren't you still
In the desert,
So I can come
Dry up my tears
Or toss them
To a watering hole
For rodents?
Why did you leave
The warmth of the sun, only
To end up in
The frozen north?
The cold will only
Preserve my despondency
I want to melt,
Molten as lava,
Yet; I am as cold
As ice
If you were still
In the desert,
I could visit
And let the sun
Leave behind
Naught but
The salt of my tears

© *25 March 1983*

    Yet when the plane landed and she stepped out into the loving arms of her family, location no longer mattered. Phoenix was free! At least, she was physically free. Now her body could begin to heal, the bruises could fade, and the memories could become bittersweet. Certainly that was what she thought as she sat in her parents' car, returned to the mid-west from the cold east coast. No doubt that was what she hoped.

Many hours later, when Phoenix followed her parents into their home, the telephone was ringing. Her husband wanted her back. The Judo instructor from base had allowed Phoenix to break free, but as soon as he felt that enough time had passed, he called her husband to tell him that Phoenix had gone. This man did not want him to "worry" too long, it seemed. According to her husband, he had been calling for hours. Apparently, the telephone had been ringing at her parent's house since just after they left home to drive to the airport to pick up their daughter.

For some time, Phoenix's husband tried to beguile her back to him. After eight years of marriage, he sent her the first bouquet of roses during the first week after she left. He called her on the telephone and begged her to come back, promising that they would have a baby. "A baby?" she thought sardonically, "What is he thinking? How in the world could he even think that was an appropriate thing to say?" Even when speaking with him on the phone, Phoenix's flight or fight response was triggered. She mustered the courage to tell him he had some audacity to offer her the enticement of a baby after all that had happened so long ago with the Princess.

He called again to tell her that he sat up all night reading the poetry she had given him over the years, and decided now that she was "quite a good little poet." In a long, flowery letter, he told her that he gathered all of her things, and made a shrine to her memory. He found God, he swore, and now he realized how badly he had treated his wife. He wanted nothing more than to apologize and set things right.

When these tactics did not work, he had his brother's ex-wife call Phoenix pretending that he had been seriously injured in a car accident. He was in the hospital asking for her, the sister-in-law insisted. Phoenix was not strong in herself yet, and this sham almost took her in. It was not easy, but Phoenix managed to hang up the telephone with a firm "No, I will not come."

She realized how fortunate she was to have such a supportive family. Her parents and siblings held her together. She survived the first few weeks. Once those first weeks had passed, she began to regain some of her own personality. Within those first few weeks, Phoenix learned to drive, got a haircut, started wearing makeup, and purchased her first automobile.

Phoenix filed for divorce and stayed where she was for the prescribed time period. Though her family moved before her divorce was final, she remained until she could attend court and reclaim her maiden name. Working for the small-town weekly newspaper as a feature writer and in the local schools as a substitute teacher, Phoenix kept busy during her wait.

When her family left the area, they headed for a more metropolitan setting in the southwest. As soon as she was able, Phoenix headed into that territory as well. She remembered the poem she had written about returning to the desert, and looked forward to living in a place where he would not be able to easily find her. In the days before the internet, it was possible to leave a life behind with the expectation of becoming someone new, at least on the surface.

The nightmares that she had been suffering had not subsided. It would be years, of course, before she would truly be able to set aside the horrifying baggage she carried. In the weeks before her divorce was final, many of her fears had turned to anger. As she drove her new car into the southwest, she recounted the past eight years of her life trying to find meaning in the chaos. She thought about how they say you see your life passing before you as you die. Perhaps she dying and about to be born into a new life. Passing a sign along the road in New Mexico, Phoenix made up a new poem. It was a song about how she felt at that very moment in time.

**Socorro by Midnight**

I left you in a steaming rage
Your hands rough with my pain
I couldn't find another song
To make it worthy my stayin'
I used to cry in long despair
And wonder what I'd done
I used to turn to you for love
'Til your hatred ruined the fun
But everything's gonna be alright
I'm gone and I ain't goin' back
Yeah, everything's gonna be alright
If I make Socorro by midnight
Years ago I felt your words
They lashed across my mind
I tried to dream my life away
But fear was all I'd find
You murdered all the love I had
In your domineering song
I prayed for change in your evil heart
But my faith couldn't be that strong
But everything's gonna be alright
I'm gone and I ain't goin' back
Yeah, everything's gonna be alright
If I make Socorro by midnight
I left you alone in your emptiness
I left you alone in your bed
You're lucky I left you alone at all
I wanted to leave you dead
But I remember the days when we used to love
The days when you seemed to care
And out of some sick respect for that
I cried when I left you there
Yeah, everything's gonna be alright
If I make Socorro by midnight.

© *1985*

She made Socorro and then some by midnight, but of course, there would be no killing. At least, no human being would be murdered. Phoenix attempted to kill the anger and fear that wrapped itself around her shriveled soul, but they were much too strong. No, she was not dying, yet. It was to be a very, very long time before Phoenix would be able to respond to life's challenges appropriately. It was as though, having already been killed herself, she was a ghost, trying to grab hold of something solid, only to find that she passed through whatever it was, leaving behind only a whisper.

# Interim 2: Back in the Mirror

*Turning on a light, I notice a movement in the glass as I wonder why the girl in the corner still cowers. Perhaps, she has moved a bit, stood up just a bit taller? I look for long moments deep into her sad eyes, searching for a sign of something, something I recognize of who I was before I was her. There – a flicker – but, no, it has passed.*

*Just in front of the cowering wraith there stands a new girl. She is another me, the one who began to emerge after the escape from the tyrant. I see now that they are tethered, she and the fearful girl-thing in the shadows. They are tethered at the ankle as if they are a chain-gang of myself. While the shadow-girl cowers in fear, the new girl is in disguise, reaching out with bloody hands and a harlequin grin. She almost seems real; she almost seems comfortable. But I know it is all an act. Oh, she is me alright – but she is still afraid; very afraid.*

## Chapter 10: Blood-Rites

It never occurred to Phoenix that it might be a good idea to get some counseling after having lived with an abusive schizophrenic for eight full years of her life. She felt powerful in her new ability to drive a car, cut her hair, and wear makeup as she wished. It was the 1980s, and Phoenix had seen MTV. In fact, the music channel had in essence saved her life. If her resolve to leave her husband had been inspired by her own realization of strength, it was galvanized by videos of strong female artists like Pat Benatar and Annie Lennox. "Hit Me with Your Best Shot" and "Would I Lie to You?" had become her internal battle cries.

During her time in the small town, Phoenix and her youngest sister had begun to model their night-out wardrobes after a controversial and fun-loving female singer by the name of Madonna. The mid-western farmers who frequented the nightspots were not sure how to take the two determined blondes in lacey half-gloves and torn up fishnet stockings. The sisters craved MTV. Their small-town cable company did not carry the channel. The two of them, along with her sister's husband, would travel to towns around the rural county whenever there was a chance to see a new band.

Most of the bands played covers of popular songs, but once in a while they would toss in an original piece to test the waters. Phoenix decided that she would try her hand at writing lyrics again for a band called Rocking Horse. They had provided a particularly fun night.

## Rocking Horse

Close your eyes and hear the sound
The sound of rock-n-roll unbound
I wonder what you wanna do
When I come rockin' in to your
Cause I'm a rocking horse, baby
Close your eyes and feel the heat
The heat of my body as I rock this beat
I wonder what you're gonna do
When I come rockin' in to you
Yeah, I'm a rocking horse, baby
(Yell) ARE YA READY TO PARTY?
I'm a rocking horse, baby
Won't ya get on and ride
This thing I feel ain't
Gonna be denied
I'm a rocking horse, baby
Hop on – let's go!
I'll take ya for a rockin' ride
Right after the show!
Yeah, I'm a rocking horse, baby
I'm a rock-n-roll man
And if ya wanna rock with me
Ya better hope you can!
Yeah, I'm a rocking horse, baby
Ya wanna go for a ride?
Think ya can handle it?
Girl, ya better decide
I'm a rocking horse baby
And I guess ya better know
I can take all you got to give!
Cause' I'm a rocking horse, baby
Yeah I'm a rocking horse, baby
I'm a rocking horse, baby
And ya better be ready to ride!

© *1 February 1986*

The band members were willing to accept the lyrics from her, but Phoenix was never to know if they did anything with them. She had read about something called a "poor man's copyright," so she mailed them to herself the day before she gave them away. The sealed envelope still sits in a drawer, yellow with age, having travelled through the years with her.

The big southwestern city was a brand-new horizon. The rock-n-roll lifestyle had intrigued Phoenix for a long time. When she was younger, she had thought that perhaps, after traipsing across Europe with her cousin and her guitar, she would be able to land a writing gig with *Rolling Stone*. At the very least, she knew she was a good enough writer to work for one of the teen fan magazines, like *Circus* or *Tiger Beat*. Now that she had been in the working world for a time, she felt she had new skills that could be useful in the field.

Phoenix believed, in her continuing naiveté, that with her talent for writing and excellent customer service skills, she would have good things to offer the music world. Not having any musical knowledge, but certainly knowing what she liked, Phoenix saw herself as a promoter or a manager. So, while she searched for "real work," she also watched for jobs that had *anything* to do with rock-n-roll. Before she even found a paying position, she found a band.

They were looking for an "all-girl" road crew, a gimmick approach to promotions. It seemed like an ideal arrangement. To Phoenix at the time, it was a dream come true. The band hired Phoenix for her enthusiasm, her writing ability, and her willingness to carry heavy objects. Working with that band for a while, she helped promote small concerts in rented dance halls, passed out promotional flyers, and carried heavy equipment. What fun she had, hanging around with musicians, partying all night, and once in a while, finding a young man to spend some time with. It seemed to be what she had imagined it to be, though without a steady paycheck, it was more hobby than vocation.

Though they did not reveal it at the time Phoenix and the other female roadies were hired, the founding members of the band were practitioners of a religion that Phoenix had not heard of before. Scientology was to become rather well known in the years to come, of course. It was not long before they began to share their religious beliefs with Phoenix and the others who worked along with her. Phoenix listened to what the band leader and his wife had to say about it and dismissed it as something she was not interested in pursuing in any depth.

Some of the other band and road crew members drifted away, turned off by this religious bent of the founders. Over time, it became clear to Phoenix that the Scientologists were not going to let the discussion drop, and that everyone who worked with them was going to be expected to convert. One day, just a day or two before Phoenix had planned on telling them she would also be ending her working relationship with them, the lead singer and his wife decided to move closer to some Scientology friends in another state and disbanded the group. Once they were gone, Phoenix never heard from them again.

With her newly found sense of freedom and adventure, Phoenix had the fortitude to apply for a job as a hostess at a strip club. There was no chance that Phoenix would have been accepted as a dancer even if she had the propensity to try, for the physical scars of her childhood burns marred the beauty of her skin. She dressed unusually for the interview, choosing a blue spandex dress that she often wore out dancing at her favorite heavy-metal nightclub, with fishnet stockings and heels.

The manager at the strip club hired her "on the spot," and she arranged to start the next day. Her job would have entailed greeting customers at the door and seating them, just as a hostess in any restaurant would do. The difference was that instead of a jazz band or other fully clothed entertainer, the stage would be populated by scantily clad and topless females. Phoenix figured that not only was it a job, it could possibly be more fun than most jobs she had held in the past.

That same day, however, she returned home to find that she had received a telephone call from another company where she had interviewed. The call was from the human resources department offering her a position that her parents would find to be more legitimate than the one she had just accepted. Not prepared to disappoint her parents after all they had done for her, Phoenix accepted the "regular" secretarial position. Almost regretfully, she called to withdraw herself from the strip club's roster.

She worked in the marketing department of a large non-profit organization. Unexpectedly, Phoenix found it difficult to concentrate on the "real world." Had she chosen to utilize her writing talents and customer service skills in the position as she should have done, she would have been successful. Unfortunately, Phoenix still had stars in her eyes and dreams of becoming a successful rock-n-roll promoter. Rather than excelling in her position as a secretary to the marketing department, she used her organizational skills in an attempt to further her dream of becoming a rock and roll promoter.

Phoenix found herself sabotaging herself on the job. She made band related telephone calls from the office, setting up appointments to present their promotional packages to venues. She set about making contacts in the music world with individuals who had been appointed to volunteer for the non-profit by court-order. She used company time and resources copying flyers and other items for concerts.

While Phoenix was guilty of using her time and talents inappropriately on the job, the problem was more than simple misplaced focus. She also felt inadequate next to her new bosses. In retrospect, Phoenix realizes that she suffered from what some call "Imposter Syndrome." She was still terrified of making telephone calls, an irrational fear that she had experienced all her life. Even the calls she made on behalf of the bands took a build-up of courage. Social anxiety and fear of being found a fraud even though she possessed the skills to excel would keep her from stepping out in confidence for years to come.

The two managers of the department where Phoenix worked were intelligent young women with degrees from Ivy League schools. Though at twenty-seven, Phoenix was older than both of them, she felt inept next to these polished, well-spoken "sorority types." She felt inadequate and shortchanged, for deep in her heart Phoenix yearned to complete her education. Her identity was still in extreme crisis. She was acutely aware that becoming a secretary had not been her idea in the first place. It had been her husband who had decided that an education in Secretarial Science was the best course for Phoenix with only two years of G.I. Bill money at her disposal. It had been her husband's desire for her to work full-time while he collected disability from the Air Force that halted her university studies.

The position at the non-profit organization lasted a month. Though she was involuntarily terminated from the position, Phoenix's experience with the institution was priceless. During her time in the job, Phoenix discovered her fear of those who had more material success and education than she possessed. She also made a new friend. At first, Phoenix had a little crush on the tall young man who had been directed to the company to serve community service. He was friendly and kind. The two hit it off as they worked side by side stuffing envelopes for fund raisers and collating hundreds of information packets and letters.

The two chatted away together, and had long talks about wonderful things. He introduced her to *The Rocky Horror Picture Show* and other bizarre creations that Phoenix had never heard of. Soon, she began to suspect that this great guy was gay, to her disappointment. When he came out of the closet to her, she was not surprised. They continued to have a good friendship, filled with laughter and the freedom to speak about anything that came to mind.

This was the first of many friendships that Phoenix would have with gay men over the next few years. Sometimes, Phoenix felt more comfortable with them than she did with women. Certainly, she was more comfortable with them than she was with straight men, whom she both desired and feared. Still, in her heart of hearts, Phoenix was lonely. She wanted someone who would love and cherish her. She found solace in rock and roll.

After she left the non-profit agency, Phoenix worked in restaurants, either serving food or cooking it. She had a fairly extensive background in the food service business, having grown up with a chef for a father and later having been a cook herself in the Air Force. The restaurant scheduling allowed more time to work with the band. It did not pay very well, however, so Phoenix continued to apply and interview for "better" jobs. During one of her interviewing rounds Phoenix met the new man in her life. She was still working with the band of Scientologists, always looking for opportunities to promote them, hoping to find good places for them to play.

She had been to a job interview for a secretarial position that morning, and was dressed quite conservatively. As she drove past a small nightclub, Phoenix noticed the name of a band advertised on the marquee. She thought it would be great idea to go inside and talk to the owner about her band. Promotional package in hand, she stepped out of her vehicle feeling a bit uncomfortable in the "normal" clothes. In Phoenix's mind at that time, anyone connected with rock-n-roll should be just a little "different." Still, she decided to give it a try. She walked into a dark, empty club and stood in the doorway looking for signs of life. A young man came into the bar through a door towards the back carrying boxes of beer. "We're closed," he said, "we open in a couple of hours."

As he emerged from the darkness, Phoenix was struck by a remarkably sensual reaction, as if a bolt of electricity coursed through her body. It was purely chemical, of course. She immediately yearned to have this man. Her first impression of him was that he looked very much like Stephen Pearcy, who was the lead singer of Ratt, a well-known rock band of the time. Like Pearcy, this young man's hair was dyed what Phoenix and her friends would come to call "fake-black," styled in a popular asymmetrical cut with one side longer than the other in front and luxurious curls hanging over his left eye. His eyes were an intense blue, his thin body well-muscled. Phoenix was suddenly, momentarily dumbstruck. She thought perhaps she would melt right there in front of him.

Once she was able to speak, Phoenix shyly introduced herself and explained why she had stopped in. The young man offered her a drink, saying that she would need to come back to speak with the owners. He was just the bar-back, setting up for the night, stocking the bar and cleaning tables. Phoenix accepted a rum and coke as a reason to stay for a while. The magnetic pull of her desire was more powerful than her fear of misstep. This was an unusual experience for her, though not quite a first. It was a feeling reminiscent of how she felt in proximity to her first love, the one she had sent away.

This man pulled out a tall bar stool, wiped it down with his cloth, and waved her toward it. She sat up to the bar as he put some music she had never heard before on the jukebox. He asked if she knew the band – the Psychedelic Furs. She told him honestly that she had not, but she liked what she was hearing. He came very close to her, and said in a whisper that made Phoenix shiver, "Come back tonight, and when I get done, maybe we can do something." The physical sensation she was feeling was now new and it was powerful. She told him she would try, but she knew she would return.

## Rockers

I walked into the rock-n-roll palace,
And there you were
Satin pants/spandex tight
Ultimate specimen of rock-n-roll reality
Foot tappin/shakin your –
High aspirations to fame
On the floor, before the stage
Playing air guitar in spaced-
Out gorgeous form (I was
Lovin' every minute of it)
My fingers ached to rake
Your thick warm hair,
A blanket full upon your shoulders
My arms ached to hold you
Tight; one night
And know your every secret,
Then: say goodbye
My body ached to dance
Before you –
A rock-n-roll princess, moving
Slowly through the palace, ready
To lay knight-ship upon a
Rock-n-roll prince like you.

© *April 1986*

Phoenix went back that night. She brought the promotional packet for the band with her, for her first order of business was to complete the quest she had begun when she stopped by the club earlier in the day. The inexplicably magnetizing young man introduced her to his bosses and Phoenix talked with them for a while. When she was done, she left the brightly lit office behind and returned to the darkened bar. A few patrons sat at tables and the bar. The bartender was a lovely dark-haired woman who laughed as she served these early arrivals. A band was setting up on stage.

As Phoenix watched the drummer set up his kit and listened to the loud music blasting from the jukebox, the young man found her a table where she could watch. He brought her a drink and invited her to enjoy the band while he worked, promising that he was looking forward to getting to know her better. She felt a new kind of power as she spent the evening listening to the music, sipping on rum and coke.

At the end of night he closed down the bar. Then, he popped open a bottle of wine and the two of them went to her car. She had parked in back of the building, where he had told her she should when they spoke earlier. They crawled into the back seat to enjoy the wine and talk. They talked for hours as they finished the wine. Eventually, they made love in the cramped space of her red sports car, never leaving the vehicle until almost dawn. Once again, Phoenix confused lust with love, and would have pursued this man into the underworld, had he asked her to. She practically did so.

She soon learned that the young man had a penchant for mainlining cocaine and drinking straight vodka once in a while. When he did, he often wanted to stay up all night and read his poetry to her. She was enthralled by him, and at first felt that she was specially chosen to be gifted by his dreamy voice and well-constructed poems. He would read his Rimbaugh-esque works and wax philosophical for hours on end. He seemed to believe that poetic angst required the impetus of narcissistic drunken reveries.

Over time, Phoenix came to understand that this "wonderful" man believed that "girl poems" were a waste of time. Phoenix would listen to his words roll from his tongue for eight or ten hours as he read from the plethora of notebooks in which he scribbled his thoughts. Yet when she wished to reciprocate with her own works, he would whisk the thought away like shooing off an annoying fly.

Phoenix would visit him at the apartment he shared with a friend. She enjoyed herself for a while, until the hours passed and she found herself thinking of food and sleep while he rumbled on, proud of his newest works. She looked forward to the evenings when they went somewhere together.

One night after the two had spent a couple of hours at the apartment, he reading from his journal as she listened, sipping on vodka and orange juice, his roommate suggested that they go out for a while. The guys knew of an after-hours club located somewhere in the industrial section of the city. They decided to go there for the evening to see what was happening.

Phoenix had not been there before and it seemed exciting to try a new place. It turned out that this place was a haven for experimental art, spoken-word performance, and hardcore punk and industrial bands. The night people frequented the place; dark vampire people, trans-people who were not yet able to come out into the light of day, gay and bi-couples, people in polyamorous relationships, and BDSM people leading one another on leashes found a home in this place. It was a place for unrestrained creativity and joy. After this first experience at this club, Phoenix was to learn to love it, and would go back many times with a female friend.

However, this first time was almost deadly. Though it was very long ago, the memory of that night remains both fearful and intriguing. The roommate drove Phoenix's car, since she had no idea where they were going and she had been drinking. Her boyfriend, in his hypo-cocaine/vodka daze, rode on the passenger side while Phoenix sat in the middle "suicide seat." As they pulled up to a parking space, her boyfriend pulled out a large jackknife that had been in his pocket.

Taking Phoenix's hand in his, he gently passed the blade over her palm. Phoenix felt no fear as it tickled across her palm, for she trusted him. Although she had been drinking some vodka and orange juice at the apartment, she was well within the limits of sobriety and fully aware of what was happening. Phoenix was certain that he only meant to tease her with the knife. It was extremely sharp, however. As he passed the knife over her palm once more, it cut her. It barely hurt as the sharp blade sliced through her skin like butter.

The cut was deep and Phoenix was bleeding heavily. She wore a large white tee-shirt (borrowed from her brother) with a maroon over-shirt, black stretch pants, and a low-slung studded belt, very 80s rock-n-roll *chic*. The three of them got out of the car, frantic to staunch the bleeding. Phoenix wrapped her hand tightly in the over-shirt. The blood kept coming. As the three of them walked quickly toward the building in search of better lighting, blood soaked the white tee-shirt. The dark red color blended with the maroon of the satin over-shirt.

For some reason, Phoenix remained calm during the ordeal, simply continuing to walk steadily toward the club looking for something else to wrap her hand in. In spite of her unnerving calm, her boyfriend was panicking, loudly apologizing to her profusely and crying. Phoenix stopped short and grabbed his arms, forcing him to stop walking. She tried to calm him down and make tell him understand that she knew he didn't mean to hurt her.

Suddenly, he pulled the knife back out of his pocket and slashed it across his own palm, cutting deep into the fleshy side below the little finger. He grabbed her hand, and holding her close, he placed his wound against hers. Together they bled for minutes, virtual hours, consoling one another. He swore that now they were connected by blood, as if this was some kind of unholy ritual. Kissing her hand, he led her to the hand-washing sink. The sink was a circular factory sink with a continuous supply of running water, like a fountain. After they washed, he took off his shirt and ripped it into strips. Then he wrapped both of their hands, finally stopping the bleeding. When it was over, Phoenix's brother's white tee-shirt was completely red with blood, dripping like water from the hemline.

After the ordeal, Phoenix fibbed to her parents about her wound. She said she had been cleaning up broken bottle glass in the dark, and put her hand down on a shard. It seemed feasible in her mind at the time. Later, her mother would tell her that she had never believed that story. Even after a week or more, the wound had still not healed properly. Phoenix's finger was swollen so large that she could not remove her ring, and the distal end was turning blue. Terrified that she might lose her finger, Phoenix went to the emergency room. It turned out that her wound required several immediate stitches and Phoenix was prescribed an antibiotic, for the wound had become infected. About two months later, she would return to the hospital for surgery to attempt a repair of the severed nerve.

As Phoenix explained to the physician what really happened, she found herself spilling out information about her defunct marriage. Perhaps it was the medication she was given for the pain, or perhaps Phoenix just needed to talk about this thing that she had kept from all of her new friends. She told the doctor about the steel-toed boots, the name calling and spitting, about the times when the entire contents of the kitchen cabinets were tossed on the floor for her to clean up while under attack. She even told the doctor about the time he had made her stand in the middle of the living room for an hour with chewing gum on her nose like a naughty third-grader because she had spent twenty cents on a pack of the stuff.

The doctor told her that perhaps it was time for her to look at a possible pattern emerging in her relationships. Phoenix heard the words the physician spoke, but she did not take it to heart. She still believed that the cut had been an accident. It had not occurred to her that had he not been an abusive type, he would not have taken the knife to her hand in the first place. The operation was not successful. The nerve that runs along the side of Phoenix's right pointer finger remains damaged and the tingling feeling will never go away.

### K 16

Love-Blood flows
Streaming madly
Mississippi-like
Never forgetting the
Ceremony of forgiveness
We once shared
Time goes by, and I
Tell myself
(As all others also tell me)
It is all for the
Best
But the scar on my soul
Has not yet healed
The river will not
Flow dry
For I
Was drowning deeply
In the current
Of your love

© *16 May 1986*

Phoenix and this man began to grow apart, yet still she yearned for him. He was a see-saw of emotional torture. He was often tender, making her believe that he honestly cared for her, but he never told her he loved her. He had been honest when he told her that he was still in love with his previous girlfriend, who had hurt him immensely. Phoenix was keenly aware of this fact, yet she honestly thought that perhaps when more time passed, he would move beyond the lost love. Perhaps, Phoenix thought, the feelings he had for *her* now could grow into love for Phoenix. However, after Phoenix had been seeing him regularly for some time, the previous girlfriend returned to his life. One day, she just showed up on his doorstep crying because she had broken up with her fiancé. From that day, he began to follow the ex-girlfriend around like a lost puppy.

Though Phoenix never learned to play guitar, she had purchased one in hopes that one day she would have the focus and drive to do so. One day, she realized that she had left her guitar at his apartment. It took two or three days for Phoenix to find the time and means to ride the bus to his neighborhood. By then, the old girlfriend had moved in with him. It was she who opened the door at Phoenix's knock. While Phoenix was not surprised to find the woman at his apartment, still her heart jumped in disappointment. She told the girlfriend that she just wanted to pick up her guitar, and she would leave.

The girlfriend smirked smugly and informed Phoenix that he had sold her guitar. Besides, said this woman who seemed unusually vindictive, he had never really liked Phoenix anyway. In fact, she told Phoenix, he thought she was ugly. Phoenix left, angry about her guitar. More importantly, she left believing that he really did think she was ugly. In retrospect, of course, Phoenix realizes that it was jealousy that prompted such vicious words from the mouth of that other woman.

Sometimes she thinks how funny it is that she had allowed the unreasonable emotions and opinions of others color her perspective of life. Taking everything that happened so seriously, Phoenix lacked the sense that might have allowed her to move forward in dignity and hope. Believing herself to be humble, she was the proverbial "doormat."

In the books she read, the women Phoenix admired most were warriors, leaders, teachers, and healers. They had a strong sense of self, a sense of humor, and an unwavering faith. Phoenix believed herself to have these qualities. If she didn't actually possess them, at least she had the imagination to survive the indignities of her life. If she didn't have the boyfriend any longer, at least she had her paper, her pen, and her muse.

### The Sale

I never thought
I'd sell my soul
And surely never
To a man
Like you –
And yet
As death has
Become the ultimate
Reality, I
Realize that sell
My soul
I have:
Love,
I sold my soul
And
You bought it for
Her

© *13 May 1986*

Phoenix saw her knife-wielding boyfriend again a year later. The beloved girlfriend had left him once again. He enticed Phoenix to meet him at his job with a promise that he truly missed her. Phoenix foolishly rejoiced that he seemed to want her after all, in spite of the other woman's words the year before. She met him after work near the university. With some of his co-workers, they entered the underbelly of the university – catacombs of pipes and drains – where they drank tequila straight from the bottle. After a while, someone decided it would be fun to go for a ride in his coworker's car.

They left the lights of the city behind, heading through the desert. As they drove, he became obnoxious, yelling at Phoenix for no reason that she could figure out. He was rude to the coworkers, who sped along the road until they were in the desert. Both coworkers, who were a couple, told him that if he did not stop behaving the way he was, he would be forced to get out of their car. Eventually, after many warnings, the driver kicked him out.

Phoenix did not need to go with him. However, because she didn't know the others, Phoenix chose to follow him into the desert. Walking across empty spaces punctuated by cacti and Palo Verde trees, he swore and spit at her. She tried to talk to him, to make some sense of what was happening. He didn't seem to hear her. When Phoenix realized that he was not going to respond to her questions, she belatedly decided it was time to leave. She turned away from him, leaving him in the desert. She headed back toward the road and hitchhiked home, almost fifty miles away.

Many years later, Phoenix would hear of him at a poetry reading. She had read a poem dedicated to him at a reading at a coffeehouse in the city, using only his first name. After the reading some people from the audience approached her, and asked if the poem referred to a certain man of the same first name. They knew him by her words, by the sensations they felt at her response to his behavior.

The world is a small place in some ways. Though it had been many years since the night Phoenix had left this man in the desert, she was to see him again just a few weeks after that reading. She had arrived a little early for the next poetry reading, so she purchased a cup of tea and sat outside at a picnic table. The café was a gathering place for 12-Step members as well as artists, poets, and young-to-middle-aged urban dwellers. As she sat savoring her hot tea in the waning afternoon, she looked up and saw a familiar face. She spontaneously called to him, and he came to sit across from her.

They sat together for a bit. He had come to the venue to attend a Narcotics Anonymous meeting which had just ended. Her heart remembered the old feeling – the yearning that she had once had for him. Now, he was struggling for sobriety. He was hungry and broke. He wanted her to buy him food. Even after so long, she would have done so if she had been able.

Though it should have been clear from his evident lifestyle that he was unable to care for another person, Phoenix gave him her telephone number, thinking that perhaps he had changed. He called her one time after that. Enlightened by the telephone conversation in which he made it clear that he was seeking codependent financial and emotional support, she changed her phone number.

## K – Epilogue One

Moons and suns and stars
Have passed,
Have burst and died
Since last we shared
A common passion –
I dreamed of you:
Betimes you were my
Night-Daemon, you
Who tore my soul,
Who ripped my flesh,
Who bled with me, Brother-
Daemon, life swirling, mesmerizing
Flowing as one:
Together, together, together
Apart forever.
Soul-Mate?  One of many –
Are we destined to be tied to
Anger, drunken poet passion,
Or can we now be friends?

*© 11 August 1995*

## To The Guitarist

I have found
I have a soul; it raises up
Each time you stroke
Your guitar and I
Am moved – with shivers
Running; tingling in time
With your ever gentle touch
Along my neck ---
      Your neck –
           The neck of your guitar
Each deep-bent string of steel
Becomes my heart, and I
Can feel the soaring
Of the ecstasy you play
In me
It stays in me
A sleeping dream,
Awakened by the astral touch
Your music has
Upon my mind

© *26 September 1985*

# Chapter 11: Phoenix and the Rock Star

After Phoenix and her demon lover split up, he lost his job at the nightclub. Phoenix happened to be at the club the day he was terminated. The owners gave her the opportunity to work with them, helping to book bands as well as cleaning the bar. It was not a high paying job, but it allowed Phoenix to pursue her outrageous dream of being a rock-n-roll promoter and provided her with free drinks when she was off duty.

While working one night, she met some men who had booked a concert to benefit a local food bank. Phoenix struck up conversation with one of them, and so began her real adventures in rock-n-roll. The conversation led to a volunteer position working with the company while continuing to work at the nightclub. Phoenix worked very hard, writing Public Service Announcements for benefit concerts and driving around town to all the local radio stations to deliver them. The hope was that if the announcements were hand-carried to the stations, they would have a good chance of getting airplay. As part of her job with this small promo company, Phoenix began booking bands into clubs other than the one she worked at. She eventually began to work as a greeter at the benefit shows, taking cover charges at the door, acting as security, and providing stage management.

The original company split after a while, and Phoenix continued to work with one of the men whom she had befriended the day she first met them. Their partnership worked well for some time, and they booked many benefit concerts into the club where Phoenix worked, another popular well-known club directly across the street, and at the large heavy metal rock nightclub across town.

Phoenix had a great time working with the bands. Eventually, the promotions added punk bands, spoken word performers, and acoustic artists to what had originally been a list comprised of all "big hair" metal bands. Phoenix and her partner had the opportunity to meet artists who were on the verge of becoming shooting stars.

At one point, they were in negotiations with an extremely popular "glam rock" band to play one of their benefit shows. After a number of preliminary talks with the band's agent, they were ready to set a date and time for the concert. Unfortunately for Phoenix and her partner, during their talks, the band signed a contract with a big record company. The band's new contract precluded work outside the recording company. It was disappointing for Phoenix, but nevertheless, she was excited for the members of the band, whom she had liked, believing them to be nice people.

Not long after this, a monolithic rock band came to town for a show at the coliseum in the city. The large heavy metal night club that Phoenix frequented was a gathering place for rock musicians whenever they were in town before a gig. As a result, the night before the concert a couple of members of the famous band came to jam with the local musicians. Knowing that the presence of the star bassist and drummer could create havoc backstage, some local band members asked Phoenix and her partner to help work security. In lieu of payment, the two were invited to attend an after-hours party at the hotel where the famous musicians were housed for the night.

The request had come on short notice, so Phoenix had been unaware that she would be asked to work. That day Phoenix had been inspired to dress up for the evening. Rather than her usual casual rock attire, she had donned a beautiful blue dress, pantyhose, and low-heeled shoes. It was more a more conservative style than most women would wear to a rock club. It certainly wasn't the clothing one would expect someone working security to wear.

Dressed as she was, Phoenix felt a bit out of place among the be-Spandexed blonde bombshell groupies and "wanna-be" rocker boys with hair lacquered with more hairspray than she could ever use. They had ended up in the bass player's room at the hotel. The entire band was in the room, except the lead singer, who travelled with his wife and was not feeling well. A few members of the local band who had shared the stage that night were in attendance, as were a handful of Phoenix's friends who worked with the promo company. The party was loud and raucous. Hotel security interrupted numerous times. Each time the security guard knocked on the door to tell them to turn the music down, the bass player would say, sure, yes. He would turn the music down, but as soon as the guard was out of sight, he would turn it up again.

In the midst of the chaos, Phoenix sat ladylike in her dress, talking quietly with her friends and others. Perhaps it was her unusual demeanor that drew the famous bass player to her, for he pulled up a chair next to the couch where she sat and struck up a conversation. When everyone left, including those who had ridden in her car with her, Phoenix was still there, spending the night with a rock star.

Later, he offered her backstage passes to his concert that night. She graciously turned down the offer. In Phoenix's mind, taking such a gift in return for a night together would have been tantamount to prostitution. She spent the night with him because she found him attractive, not in order to get something from him. She had not been star-struck, but had simply enjoyed his company. Phoenix left quietly in the morning. As she left the hotel, she stopped by the front desk to leave a note. She would never know if he understood her reasoning, or if he appreciated her honesty.

Phoenix has felt a great amount of guilt when she has thought about that night. It would be dishonest to pretend that this guilt has anything to do with having had a "one night stand" with the famous bassist. The main regret that Phoenix has had is that her mother could not reach her when she attempted to call her that night. There were no cell phones in those days. Messages left at the club were never delivered, and after the group left for the hotel, there was no way for anyone to reach them. Phoenix will always regret not taking the time to check in with her parents, for that was the night Phoenix's grandfather passed away.

### ChristSonnet

Once He forgave the Magdalene;
In Damascus, He called to Paul
The miracle, though: He forgave me too
And I'm the least one of all
Although I have sinned
A million sins
And am bound to sin so much more
Our Lord has given all for me:
As for His Disciples before!
Like John, who was the most beloved
As Thomas, who wanted to doubt
With Lydia's purple passionate praise,
I pray to share what He's about

For had I been there, with Magdalene
Would I have felt that I was clean?

© *4 February 1985*

## Chapter 12: Rock-n-Roll Reality

Phoenix's life had become a walk along a thin precipice. Sometimes she felt as if she was inching along a narrow path barely wide enough for her to put one foot in front of the other. She imagined that if she fell, on one side she would be dashed against jutting rocks; on the other, she would be lost in a dark, deep abyss. Teetering along the edge, she neared disaster in more ways than she recognized at the time.

Her job at the bar provided the benefit of free drinks when she was off duty, and she never hesitated to take advantage of that benefit. Her boyfriend had gone off with his previous girlfriend, leaving Phoenix single once again. Later, she would know that she should have sought out counseling after leaving her husband. She had been so damaged by her experiences in the Air Force and the spousal abuse that it would take years for her to recover. Counseling might have expedited the process. Instead, she had entered into a rock-n-roll dream. In truth, it might have actually been a nightmare.

Emotionally, Phoenix was a mess. She rode extreme highs, feeling she was "in love," with one guy or another. Usually, the object of her affection was unattainable. She wrote poems of unrequited "love" for men she barely knew. She was aware that these were simply "schoolgirl crushes," yet somehow, she convinced herself that they were something deeper, more profound. During this time, Phoenix found temporary emotional fulfillment in short-term relationships and one-night stands. One night, a band of mid-level fame with one hit on the music channel MTV played at the club where Phoenix worked. Phoenix was off-duty that night, so she received a few free drinks for herself and her closest friends.

People gathered around her table. In the reverberating beat of rock and roll, she felt popular. At some point, however, Phoenix left the party with someone, though later she had no recollection of the other person's identity. Hours later, she awoke in an extremely dark place, wearing nothing but her pants. Her glasses were missing, and she could not find any other clothes. Not knowing where she was, Phoenix inched her way in the darkness to find a way outside, moving slowly toward a sliver of light. As she reached the source of the light, she found large plate glass windows, painted black. The light was streaming weakly through a broken window in the corner. Almost blindly, she stepped through the broken window into the clear dark night to find that she was standing outside an empty store just around the corner from the bar. Not having found her top, Phoenix crossed her arms in front of her against the cold December night and was forced to find a pay telephone so she could call the police to help her.

Standing on the parking lot shivering, arms wrapped around her shirtless body, barefoot and blind without her glasses, Phoenix felt a sense of hopelessness and fear. Who had she left with? She had no memory of talking to anyone other than her friends. How did she end up in such a position? She was aware that she had downed a few drinks, but surely, she had not had enough to cause her to black out -- had she? At the time, Phoenix did not know about date-rape drugs, though in retrospect, she realized this was the likeliest answer to this mystery.

When the police arrived, she was given a blanket to wrap herself in. The officers were kind, but she could not help but sense an underlying accusation. She could not tell the officers anything about who had left her in the store, nor could she say what had happened, for there was no memory of anything from the time she was laughing with her friends and the moment she opened her eyes in the dark half naked. The officers drove her to the border of the town where she lived, where another officer met them. Phoenix moved from one patrol car to another, and was taken home.

That night scared her. For a time, she stopped drinking completely. A friend of hers was attending Narcotics Anonymous meetings at the time. Rather than go alone to Alcoholics Anonymous meetings, Phoenix went with her friend to the NA group for a while. She was not the only young person who chose to attend Narcotics Anonymous for a perceived alcohol problem. They felt more comfortable opening up to what seemed to be a younger group. The stories she heard terrified Phoenix. She felt that she would never drink again, and for a long time, she turned down even a glass of wine. After a few years, she did begin to drink socially once more, but never again did she have an experience like the one she had that night.

Now, 'way back in the time that Phoenix was awaiting the finalization of her divorce, she had contacted her first love, the young man she asked to leave when she was still a teenager. He had been married, as she had, but was single again as well. She called the long-distance operator and got his parents' phone number. He was living in the southern part of the U.S., living with a sibling. Once Phoenix reached him, the two began a series of long telephone conversations and letter exchanges. Since his divorce, he had been injured in a hitchhiking accident. When Phoenix found him at his sibling's home, he was bedridden while he healed from his extensive injuries. He spent two years recuperating.

In the days when Phoenix had been married, there had been many times when she had felt as if this man was nearby. She attributed the sensation to her strong imagination, and constructed stories and poetry about him, never expecting to see him again in real life. During their long telephone conversations as she awaited her divorce court date, he told her that he and his wife had lived in the same state Phoenix had lived in during her marriage. He had been only miles away when she had the sensation of his close proximity.

The serendipity of this seemed like a metaphysical gift. Phoenix was certain it was no coincidence, and that the two of them were ordained to be connected to one another for all time. It wasn't as if she had expectations of their earlier romance rekindling. This had been her mentor in the spiritual pursuits of her burgeoning adulthood. It had always seemed that they had known one another over many lifetimes, and the knowledge that her sense of his closeness was correct confirmed this for Phoenix. Once she arrived in the southwestern city, she wrote to him with her new address. They maintained an intermittent pen-pal relationship. She thought of him often, and could usually anticipate when a letter would arrive.

Weeks after the alcohol scare, Phoenix began working with another band, this time a heavy metal group with some very talented musicians. Around the same time that she entered this new endeavor, Phoenix had taken a job at a chain restaurant, working the bar-rush shift. Phoenix moved into an apartment with one of her sisters and her children. In their teen years, her sister had also been close friends with Phoenix's first love. One night, as Phoenix prepared for work, her sister told her she had the feeling their old friend was going to be around soon. Phoenix had not yet had the time to send a letter to her old flame with her new address, but was thinking of doing so in the next day or so. She wanted to laugh when her sister insisted that she was certain he would be there soon. How could he come see them? He didn't know where they lived! Her sister was right.

Two weeks after her sister shared this insight, as Phoenix was once again preparing for work, there was a knock upon the door. Phoenix's sister opened the door – and there he stood! Now, neither of the women had seen this man since they were in their teens. As her sister stood in the doorway, holding open the door for him to enter, Phoenix turned. There was no doubt that it was him. She stood a moment, looking upon a much older version of the man whom she had first loved. He was slightly twisted from the accident, but was still attractive in the way that first drew Phoenix to him. Now, however, they were destined to be friends rather than lovers. For a time, it seemed they might be business partners.

This man, the "Heathcliff" of Phoenix's earlier poem, had received a settlement as a result of his accident. When he arrived in the city, he was still awaiting the payout. By the time it arrived, he had decided to invest some of it into the new band that Phoenix was working with. He rented a house and they all moved in, providing a regular practice venue for the band. Soon another band joined the household for regular practice. The house was a cacophony of constant partying, and a gathering of girls – band girlfriends, groupies, and guests.

It had become evident to Phoenix by this time that she and her first love were not to become a couple. Still lonely, she sought a relationship, imagining a day when she would find someone to spend the rest of her life with. Of course, she still was not properly equipped to recognize a potential life partner. She chose her objects of affection by her physical response to their presence. If a man responded positively to Phoenix in any way, she was enamored.

Among the guests who came to the house there was one young man that Phoenix was attracted to. He was nice to her, and his sense of humor made her light-hearted. The two began to talk into the night about the many subjects that interested Phoenix. They found they had much in common. They had a wonderful time together, and because he treated her nicely, she fell in love.

Momentarily, Phoenix felt happy. She had not asked him any questions, so she was unaware at first that this man was a few years younger than she was, nor that he was in a relationship with someone else. They talked for hours, and when he fell asleep in the wee small hours of the morning, Phoenix wrote a poem. He inspired in her thoughts of Greek gods. Smitten, she did not want to forget this moment, in which he lay stretched out with the light of the full moon illuminating his wild red curls and his alabaster, freckled skin.

## Angelic

A longtime lonesome spot
Was filled last night
But who knows how long
It can last?
A moment's rushing pleasure
Never promises more than
Ecstasy unleashed
And the child-like grasp
Of a plaything
I could care for you
If I could know you
But just to hold you
Would be enough
Yet tonight I'm alone,
My fingers remember
Soft curves and the
Tangle of hair across
My face: I think of you
The moonlight falls
Blue upon the empty
bed beside me,
And right now, I simply wish
that you were here

*© 8 January 198*

He stayed at the house with Phoenix and her roommates for a few days. Then one morning, his girlfriend arrived to pick him up. By that time, Phoenix knew about the girlfriend. She knew that he would never be hers. He and Phoenix were to remain friends for some time though neither of them could know for how long. After the rock-n-roll days ended, they lost touch with one another. Unexpectedly, they would come across each other in later life; each disappearing into the world without a goodbye, then appearing like specters from one another's pasts unannounced every ten years or so.

Phoenix no longer held an outside job, but neither was she booking bands and promoting shows. At the band house, Phoenix had suddenly become the maid, cook, and all-around mother figure. In truth, it almost wasn't fun anymore. Then, the bass player for the band asked her out on a date. Phoenix had rotated her "crush" feelings between two of the band members and another friend who lived in the house, none of whom saw her as anything but a useful girl to have around.

This man, the bass player, was not Phoenix's usual "type." He was a big man, good looking, and tender. He was the "teddy bear" type. The two began dating and soon he was considering Phoenix his girlfriend. He did not live in the house, but came only to practice or hang out. He would come and treat Phoenix with respect, like a woman, and take her to dinner. In the meantime, life at the house became unbearable for Phoenix. She felt used, unappreciated, and depressed.

One day, she packed up a few important items and ran away from home, telling no one she was leaving. After she had been gone for a few days, staying with a friend, Phoenix thought she should let the people at the band house know where she had gone. She had begun to think they were probably concerned about her. She called her beloved "Heathcliff," for they had been friends for the longest time.

In her imagination, Phoenix thought perhaps he would come in like a knight and sweep her off her feet like a princess of old. She dreamed he might beg her to come home, tell her he loved her more than anyone he had ever loved. Perhaps she hoped he wanted her to come back to the house and be with him happily ever after. In her loneliness and despair, she had forgotten her earlier realization that they could not be together in a romantic way.

By this time, he was not interested in her in this way, any more than she was interested in him as a romantic partner.

For some reason she did not understand, a part of her held on to the version of him who she had fallen in love with during the summer of her seventeenth year. The version of him who had saved her during her deepest, darkest times throughout her marriage was imaginary. He did not exist in truth, and she knew this. Nevertheless, even now she held tight to the memory of the two of them as they once were.

Now, he did not sweep her off her feet, but he did beg her to return to the house. They needed her there, he claimed, for there was no one there to do the laundry and wash the dishes on a regular basis. The guys in the bands only cared for the space to practice. Phoenix decided not to go back to the house to live. Whether this was a decision of practicality or the result of her confused and broken heart, Phoenix will never know for sure.

In truth, the man she had fallen in love with when she was seventeen was not interested in pursuing a romantic relationship with anyone, let alone Phoenix. Instead, he was caught up in the possibility of fame and had immersed himself in the rock-n-roll lifestyle. After all, it wasn't so very different from the hippie lifestyle he led when Phoenix asked him to leave so many years before.

Though he was no knight in shining armor, Phoenix still loved him in her own way. She still loves him, will always love him in a way only the girl who remembers being seventeen can love. It isn't the kind of love one can build a relationship on. Rather, it's the kind of love that makes up dreams for lonely women who consider the past and believe that the best of life has passed them by. For this was who Phoenix had become.

She was not yet thirty years of age, but she felt as though she had reached her zenith years before. She believed she had given her soul to the men who had broken her, and something deep inside her cried out to be rescued. Perhaps that broken soul could be repaired by traveling back in time to the day she walked across a grassy park on a college campus with her sister, the day she shared a bottle of Chianti with a group of hippies and fell in love with the tall Nordic blond who first loved her.

### Soul-Mate

You are my beloved
Always have you been
A part of my heart
We must have been made
Together, you and I
Twin souls, God's children
Once one and the same
Yet sundered early,
Ravaged by this physical life
Torn by birth and Destiny
My heart is wrenched in
Loneliness when I think
Of you, and my soul
Wanders the landscape
Of dreamtime
Alone until the day
That you and I find
One another
Once more

© *18 August 1999*

## Chapter 13: The Girl in the Song

Once Phoenix had moved away from the band house, she found refuge in a downtown alternative art gallery. It was the advent of a new era in Phoenix's adventurous life. She was given a private bedroom in the back of the house. In exchange, she organized poetry readings for art openings. The house was a gathering place for artists, writers, poets, and revolutionaries.

The gallery was a hub of *avante-garde* activity; Phoenix was ecstatic to be part of the great energy generated around the openings. An art exhibit usually opened in the evening, with a wine and cheese event, a band playing on the stage in the back yard, and eclectic poetry readings. These readings were very different from the kind of event where Phoenix had read while she was married. These readings may have been an early precursor to the poetry slam, which evolved later. It was during this time period that rap was developing as an acceptable art form, punk music was peeking its head out of the dark alternative and into the mainstream. The readings at the gallery represented a transition point between the beat and the street.

One artist who often worked and showed his works at the gallery was a painter whose style was more like graffiti than fine art. In fact, one of this artist's arguments in the community was that local artists should be represented in the major galleries alongside famous masters. He was a graffiti artist, to be sure, but he also used canvas in the same way he used the walls of the city. The artist's subject matter included road kill, a commentary on the darkness of the human condition. Phoenix was intrigued by him, as was her friend Lavender. He was a kind soul who had suffered horrible abuse as a child, and so was empathetic to the struggles of these women who sought healing from the violence of their marriages.

## Artist

He is Everywhere
Ubiquitous Anger
Slashed red and black
Across the canvas
Of the city –
Truth tastes bitter,
He spits it back
For all the world to see
Repulsed, they reject him
And hope he'll crawl away
A trodden worm, to hide
Beneath a rock
But anger like his
Cannot be buried
Death's Head must fly
To announce the thievery
Reality has rent upon the world'
Thrashed violently by the
Winds of change
He isn't afraid, nor am I
Those who do not Fear
Find refuge in One Another,
And his Anger attracts me
I'm in love

*© 23 February 1987*

Phoenix's poetry had become angry during the preceding months. It was dark and brooding; it seethed with the frustrations begotten by unrequited love and un-realized dreams. Phoenix's words reflected her own roller-coaster emotions, superimposed with heavy metal and hardcore punk-rock politics. The artists who shared the space at the gallery were inclined toward the dark as well. In the space that was once a kitchen in a charming home, a huge interactive art piece thrust the visitor into an imaginative post-nuclear time warp. A black baby crib, reminiscent to Phoenix of a Sylvia Plath poem, sat within a 1950's retro-room left as if the bomb had dropped, annihilating the inhabitants and leaving all else frozen in Pompeii-esque stasis. Inside the crib, an antique record player was set to replay Black Sabbath's "War Pigs" endlessly in a scratchy, warped loop of doom. Upstairs, a female artist and taxidermist created unique furniture pieces comprised of dead animals, stuffed and wrapped around lamps and chicken skulls cleaned and mounted inside glass table tops.

Most of the artists who displayed their works at the gallery lived elsewhere. They arrived for the opening party and revisited their works throughout the show period, bringing along their friends. There were a handful of artists who temporarily stayed in the gallery along with their works while Phoenix and one or two others had their own rooms in the house. It was an arrangement that provided home for misfits like Phoenix as well as live-in security for the house.

Phoenix kept her private room available for visitors most of the day, closing the doors and locking them only when she was sleeping. As a result of this open-door policy, her walls became artworks in themselves. Visitors to the gallery often wandered into her room, leaving their signatures, poetry, and thoughts upon the walls. If Phoenix was in the room, they would often stay and talk with her. She invited friends over to visit and share her ear, her time, and her thoughts.

For a time while she lived in the gallery, Phoenix continued dating the bass player. At first, she didn't realize that he considered her his girlfriend. In her mind, they were just "seeing one another." Without a verbal agreement to be exclusively his steady girlfriend, she continued to allow herself to become sidetracked by attractions to other people. One evening this kind man took her to a popular blues club to meet with some of his friends and family. Without warning, he introduced her as his girlfriend, then turned to her and asked if it was okay with her that he had done so. Phoenix as taken by surprise. She felt she had no recourse but to agree. She nodded, oblivious to the fact that by acquiescing to this introduction, she was accepting the role and would be expected to behave as such.

Not long after this, Phoenix went to the rock-n-roll club with her friend Lavender. That night they met some men there who wanted to show them a good time. Phoenix and Lavender chose not to leave the club with the men; however, Phoenix walked one of them to his vehicle. When they reached the car, the young man pulled Phoenix close and gave her a kiss. He was attractive, and Phoenix had enjoyed a drink or two while at the club. She kissed back, then turned away and rejoined her friend inside the club.

Unknown to her, one of the bass player's friends happened to be in the parking lot at the time. He reported that Phoenix was "cheating" on the bass player. It was only when the bass player confronted Phoenix about the incident that she realized that she had accepted the commitment. After a long discussion, she accepted his request to see him exclusively. They dated for a few months, enjoying the sights and sounds of the city.

With this kind man, Phoenix had dinner at fine restaurants. Sometimes he would call her on the phone at the gallery and ask her to go out on short notice. During this time in her life, Phoenix was rarely without plans to do something in the evening. When he would call her expecting to take her out on the same night, she often had already made plans to do something with Lavender. Rather than forego seeing Phoenix, he would invite Lavender to join them. The three would take in a film or a nice dinner after which he would drive Lavender to the apartment where she lived before talking Phoenix back to the gallery.

One of Phoenix's best memories of her time with this great bear of a man was the night he picked her up and took her for a drive. Refusing to tell her his plans for the evening, he drove her to a large park that included a man-made lake. He parked, then walked around the car to open Phoenix's door for her. Then he took a basket out of the trunk of the care and led Phoenix to a place near the lake. He spread a cloth upon the grass and proceeded to lay out an elaborate picnic dinner. They sat together under the stars, enjoying the clear, star-studded desert night, sipping wine and talking. It was a very romantic setting. That evening would always be a fond memory for Phoenix.

Although Phoenix truly enjoyed her time with this man, she was not ready for a long-term relationship. He knew she had been married before, but Phoenix was unable to tell him how badly the marriage had gone. She was as yet unaware of the full extent of the damage she had incurred during her married. Lavender was the only person she could confide in, for she herself had escaped a similar situation. Eventually, Phoenix felt she could not continue to allow the bear of a man to think there was a possibility that their relationship might evolve into something deeper. Since he had shifted their relationship to exclusive, she would have to break up with him This was something she could not do in person. It felt too much like confrontation to a woman who feared it. Instead, She wrote him a break-up poem, hoping it was gentle and that it truly reflected her desire to keep the friendship that had begun when she first started working with the band.

Many people seem to consider the idea that a woman who does not want to date someone anymore but who wishes to remain friends is intentionally being hurtful. Often this is not the case. It was certainly not the case for Phoenix. The reality for Phoenix is that even as she has felt the need to break a man's heart, her heart was breaking as well. It is no small thing to realize that one must be hurtful in order to do the right thing. Phoenix was beginning to realize that she had to undergo much more healing in order to transcend the abusive situation that she had only recently escaped. She had no idea at the time how much healing she had to undergo, for she had not yet realized the impact of her experiences in the Air Force. It would be many, many years before she knew exactly what had happened.

By the time Phoenix reached her twenty-ninth birthday, she had written the break-up letter to her bass player boyfriend. Since leaving her husband, Phoenix had been unable to commit to a long-term relationship. The punker with the drug problem had been her first and longest-term lover in the time since her divorce. Phoenix and her bass player had been "an item" for a very short time. He treated her too well, respected her too much. After eight years in her previous married life, Phoenix just didn't know how to act with a man who actually cared about her. After breaking up with him she set out to find the next passionate and exciting love of her life.

After the break up, which he took surprisingly well, he wrote a song about her. One night when Phoenix went to a house party to see the band play, he sang it. Her heart was wrenched at the pain she had caused, but it was a good song, and she felt a strange mixture of shame and pride at hearing it. She recalls to this day leaning against a wall, headbanging to the heavy metal riffs the guitarist placed between the words of heartache and the deep bass-line played by the very man whose heart she had broken. The guilt she felt then is awakened even now, for though she knows she could not have committed herself to him, she never explained the reasons why.

Later in life, Phoenix hoped to see him again and to apologize for her behavior. She still had never explained to anyone other than Lavender what kind of marriage she had left. She thought she was being completely honest with the men she dated, but she had not been able to reveal the details of her past with them nor with other friends who she felt could not understand her experience. Though she was never intentionally dishonest, the omission of full disclosure helped to create the illusion to the bass player's friends that she had just used him. As she matured, gathering new experiences and insight, she realized the truth of what she had done.

Years later, Phoenix was in his old neighborhood dropping off some donated clothing to an organization nearby. She stopped in a convenience store for a cold drink. Heading back to the refrigerators, she passed by a large man who seemed familiar. Their eyes met, and she almost cried out his name. However, she was unsure if it was him. It had been so long, and this man was much bigger than he had been, yet deep in her heart she thought it was him. Afraid to be wrong, she didn't speak. Her regret was compounded when, a few years after this encounter, she connected with another member of his old band and asked about him. The guitarist told her that he had been stricken down by an early heart attack, leaving behind a wife and children.

Sometimes, regret never ends.

## The Girl in the Song

I was once the girl in the song
Nothing to be proud of, there
My name penned into verse
Hammered heavy-duty
Hardcore
Thrash, metallic
Guitar riffs.... all
Because I hurt someone
I didn't mean
To hurt
He was a nice guy
And I, I was a lonely girl
Lost in my own transgressions
Faced with my unspoken confusion –
I knew not who I was;
Knew nothing of what
I wanted, following only
Where my aching heart and my
Empty soul would lead
I was the girl in the song
And he who penned it has passed away
Into the next world, too young
Leaving behind a girl
Who loved him and children
Who probably never knew
Their dad wrote a song
About a girl who was not their mom
He's gone and the song lost;
And I am a girl
Who, looking back, wishes
She was the girl in a song
Where the number was lost
Before the heartache
Could begin

*© 29 August 2008*

## Chapter 14: Elf-Witch

During the time Phoenix lived at the art gallery, she looked forward to the nights when a new art exhibit would open. While not all of these opening parties included a poetry reading before the musicians played, most of them did. Phoenix would always read her own works and introduce the other poets and speakers.

When Phoenix worked with the bands, she often went on stage to introduce them or make announcements. Under stage lights, Phoenix could rarely actually see the audience. It was easier for her to overcome her fear of rejection talking into a microphone in front of an invisible crowd. Poetry was a little different. The venue was smaller, and she felt vulnerable. To overcome her fears, she had taken to putting on a foreign persona for readings. Donning a hooded gauze dress that she had redesigned by cutting the skirt into jagged edges, with sleeves long and flowing, like gossamer wings, Phoenix felt like another kind of creature. She teased out her hair – black and blonde intermingled – and placed the hood over her head. This night, as she dressed, she proclaimed herself "Elf-Witch," She felt like maybe she could make her dreams come true.

**ElfWitch's Wishsong**
...Then she remembered those who
She called "friend," and who
Had taken her hand –
When all along it was her
Freely offered love they
Chose to steal.
Betrayed, she called upon
The winds to save
Her name...
And windsong came...

*© 1987*

One particular party seemed to promise a new horizon for Phoenix. The event that evening was held outdoors, with poets and musicians performing from a makeshift stage in the backyard. Though it was an art opening, this one was different from most. Rather than the usual fare of wine, cheese, and jazz, this event featured an extravaganza of offerings from various cultures, pot-luck style. The music was to be experimental rock and industrial *avant-garde*, with a final performance piece featuring cello, bass, and violin players dancing around a fire. It was the perfect night for Phoenix to claim her persona of mystery and strength. She turned herself into Elf-Witch and proceeded to give a speech about artistic freedom and read some of her angriest poetry.

### The Speech

*Hi, I'm Phoenix and I'm a creator. You know, in the last year I've totally alienated my family because I've been so busy creating my own clique that I've been ignoring the one they bequeathed to me. Yeah, me and my closest friends, we're the Heavy Metal Valley Punk Thrashers of America (Like, fer sure, F\*n A!) We're the thrash/glam/punk queens of rock-n-roll and we're ready to tell the world what's different about us. So, what's different about us? NOTHING.*

*There's absolutely nothing different between us and punk-thrash-metal-glam-reggae-art-poetry-nude modeling. All we do is knock down the barriers built around our freedom of expression. We are all in it to share the same fears-hates-loves-desires and leather and lace and a made-up face could say it as well to some as black widow weeds and a death mask. The new '80's movement is just a re-generation of the 60's anti-war rap, and peace-love-day glo smiles and flowers won't work anymore so we punctuate with black-white-death-skulls-weaponry and angry sounds colored here and there with glam glitter neon, like the last glimmers of hope in a doomed existence.*

*So, if we're gonna die a nuclear death anyway, we might as well destroy the world as we know it first and create a new one. It is through our own forms of expression that this revolution occurs, and it will occur only as fast as we have the guts to punch the world in the stomach with their own realities.*

*So, whatever your reality is -- whatever your medium of expression is, be it music, words, fashion, art, whatever - don't be afraid to shock the world with it. Only those who risk their security, their comfort and their reputation <u>ever</u> actually hurdle those barriers that were placed in the pathway to individuality.*

© 1987

In her own way, Phoenix as Elf-Witch was an activist, a militant female artist claiming the right to religious and artistic freedom. She was successful, if even for that one night, for at the end of the show, she was invited to perform her work on a video which the producers claimed would feature "hard core poets of Phoenix." They told her that she was the only female invited to perform on this video. *Just think,* Phoenix mused to herself, *I never thought of myself as hardcore!*

Only a year before her boyfriend, he of the blood-rites, had told her that if she wanted to be punk, she should do something drastic like shave her head. At the time, she declared she *didn't* want to "be punk." She *wanted* to be herself, whatever that was. In Phoenix's mind, this invitation to be included in a video of "hardcore poets" was even better than shaving her head could possibly have been.

However, like so many other times, she passed on the opportunity. Phoenix was afraid of many things in those days. The experience with her husband had placed her on tenterhooks; if she felt the slightest sense of foreboding, she would react negatively. If she was living a life of bohemian adventure, it was not a solitary life. She had a friend with her most of the time. Usually, Lavender was along for the ride. In this case, she was invited to a studio in the city, alone. Something felt wrong about it, so she didn't go.

Phoenix will never know if she sabotaged herself and ruined a once-in-a-lifetime opportunity or if she inadvertently made a wise decision. Listening to the news in today's world, Phoenix understands that women everywhere are taken and trafficked through various tricks like promises of fame and grandeur. There is a small part of her that thinks perhaps her intuition served her well that day.

Intuition notwithstanding, Phoenix had fallen into a downward spiral which took her to a rock and roll netherworld she didn't quite understand. She believed that most of the people she met at the gallery and at the clubs were her friends. After Phoenix and her bass guitar boyfriend broke up, she began to hang out with a few men that she met at the gallery. She did not date them; rather, she made friends with whom she could speak about many things. Through them, she learned a little more about the dark and seedy side of American life.

One of the poets was a thin, scruffy young man who had been a runaway when he was a teenager. He claimed that he had been a male prostitute in New York for a while. He declared proudly that one of his clients was a singer from the underground music movement of the sixties and seventies who by now was quite famous. Phoenix didn't doubt the young man's stories. She found him fascinating, and his ambiguous sexuality was part of the attraction. The two of them started gathering with a few other poets for readings and discussion. The group didn't last long, for the young man's pursuit of illicit hypodermic kits and the contents for which they would be used demanded his attention. As a result, he was invited to stop frequenting the gallery.

Another of her new friends lived across the street from the gallery. He was a slightly disturbed young artist who shared an apartment with two other men. Phoenix and Lavender befriended them all and took to hanging out at their apartment periodically. The apartment belonged to an older man who seemed to the girls as nice enough, but he appeared to wish they would not come over to visit so often. Nothing was ever really said to either of the women about this; rather, there was a strong sense that they were rushed away whenever he was home or expected home.

There was a strange and mysterious atmosphere about the apartment. It was just a small, second-story apartment. However, whenever Phoenix and Lavender walked past the building on the west side, they had the feeling that they were being watched. Looking up at the bathroom window, they always felt as if they could see a dark, rather opaque *being* standing there, looking at them with red, glowing eyes. There was a sense of evil that permeated the air around the apartment building. Soon it became difficult for the two young women to climb the stairs to the apartment. With each step up the grated staircase, the sense of foreboding became more palpable. They were unwilling to give in to the fear that grew in their hearts, so they kept going in spite of it. They began to say the Lord's Prayer aloud in unison as they went.

Even when they no longer spent time with "the boys," Whenever Phoenix or Lavender passed the building, they would glance up toward the bathroom window, wondering what sort of dark guardian the older man had set. Who had he been, this older man who took in two young men and seemed suspect of the time they spent with the two women who came to visit?

**Lost Soul**

Deathchild, Lover of disfigured
Demons Dancing
Madly, gladly, sadly across
The pains of Anger
Bloodlusting for the
Violent seduction of those who
Would rend his perfect heart
Asunder
He wished Death upon those
Who would kill a dream,
Or slash wicked wounds through
The eyes of his Artist's soul
On those who cry,
Who try, who die
Lonely and loveless
In a world that executes
Art upon a block of commercialism
And buries it deep beneath
A funereal mound of rules
That preach the holiness of
Monetary success
He cried a child alone among many
He found his dream to be too real
He'll learn that if he takes the hands
And hearts of his own kind, they'll
Share their dreams; the Nightmares
Of those who know the Truth.

© *7 March 1987*

By the time Phoenix and Lavender had befriended the young men, Phoenix was working with a hard-core thrash rock band. The red-haired "angel boy" she had met while living at the band house was the drummer. The lead singer was a startling young woman who spoke like a sweet angel and sang like a demon out of hell. In order to promote the band, Phoenix arranged a concert and heavy-metal art show at the gallery. The young artist from across the street provided a number of paintings for the art exhibit. The band set up outside, while some of the more radical of the regular gallery artists displayed their works and milled about. The show seemed to go well; yet Phoenix was distant.

In the week prior to the show, she became sick with bronchitis. There were some interpersonal difficulties between her friend and a young man, which somehow affected Phoenix's perception of the day. Phoenix was late to the beginning of the show, which angered the lead singer. Although Phoenix was clearly ill, the woman yelled at her and called her a bitch. This devastated Phoenix, who wanted everyone to like her. She was overly sensitive to those who did not like her.

When she heard about the singer calling her names, her feelings were deeply hurt. She retreated to her room, threw herself on her bed, and cried like a teenaged girl. Phoenix felt ashamed, not only because the woman had called her a bitch when she knew it was not an accurate assessment of her personality, but because she had not behaved in the way she expected herself to. Phoenix knew she had missed an opportunity to act the professional, and her emotions overwhelmed her. She avoided seeing the singer again, and for many years felt deep embarrassment at the memory.

Phoenix believed then, and still believes, that she always had good intentions, even if the results of her actions indicated otherwise. Sometimes it seemed to Phoenix that she existed in a surreal world where everything turned out the exact opposite of what one expected. She sometimes thought that this was what Alice felt like beyond the looking glass.

When Phoenix turned twenty-nine, she and her friend Lavender threw a huge birthday party. They were fans of a band from a city a few hours away. The band was booked for one night into one of the clubs the friends frequented. Since the band would be in town the night before the gig, it seemed an ideal opportunity to ask them to play for Phoenix's birthday at the gallery. The women felt lucky that the band would play their party for a mere $200.00. They hired the band and asked party-goers to pay $2.00 each to cover the cost of the band.

It was a wonderful party. The girls decorated the main room of the gallery and purchased cake and other food to satisfy hungry guests. They had no problem taking in enough cash to pay the band, which played until 2:00 am. After the party, however, things got a bit hairy. The nature of the band and the artistic surroundings were indicative of alternative lifestyles. Drugs and alcohol had made it into the gathering. Phoenix's red-haired angel friend and his girlfriend brought champagne.

Of course, Phoenix and Lavender were happy to partake in the generosity in celebration of a milestone – two years since Phoenix had left her husband, and she felt like she was a belle of the rock and roll ball! She, who had not been allowed to wear make-up, to cut her hair, or to learn how to drive was now wearing Spandex dresses, multiple earrings, and a tattoo on her left breast! She marveled at how far she had progressed in the world. This birthday represented a sense of freedom for both women, who had suffered such pain at the hands of men who had claimed to love them.

Phoenix and Lavender had met through a mutual friend and originally bonded over a shared crush on a local bass player. It wasn't long, however, before the two women realized that they had much more in common than a two-bit bass guitarist with a penchant for losing his pants in the back seat of fan-girls' cars.

Both women were survivors of abusive husbands. While Phoenix had come through eight long years with her spouse, Lavender had walked away the day her husband of two years pulled a gun in her face. Neither woman had chosen therapy – both found solace in the party atmosphere of the late 1980s heavy-metal culture. They mistakenly searched for true love among longhaired be-Spandexed rockers whose ideal women seemed to be tall, thin, bleach-blondes who towered in spike heels. Neither Phoenix nor her friend met any of these criteria. True love would prove to be hard to find.

With this party, they felt as if they had the potential for anything and everything wonderful to happen. At the direction of the gallery manager, the musicians played in the dirt basement, where fans flowed down the stairs periodically and returned above ground to dance and mill about, food and drink in hand. All the revelry proved to be too much for the live-in manager of the gallery. Phoenix had over-imbibed, and perhaps he had as well. As the night drew to a close and the band broke down their equipment, he confronted Phoenix about some issue or other – trash left in the yard or some other guest's behavior. Phoenix would forget soon after what the exact problem was. However, the argument that ensued was the catalyst for Phoenix's decision to leave the gallery. Once the band and all the guests had left, Phoenix gathered up her few belongings and moved in with Lavender.

### *Soul Food*

Rhythm fingers play upon
My strings, heart strings,
Strings of hearts of music
Rhythmic movement
Pulls me:
Cruise me, lose me,
Use me
Toss me soft upon
The futon: further
Futile resistance
Plays against your
Rhythm, won't you
Dance me, trance me,
Prance me
Slow across the floor
Prize me, spies me,
Hypnotize me
Take me to a world
Beyond, and love me
Hug me, hold me,
Take me, Make me
Play me like the
Fine-tuned tool you
Hold each night
The stars and sky
Will harmonize
And we will
Make music
Sing me, bring me
Deep within your
Hungry soul.

*(c) 10 March 1989*

# Interim 3: Through the Glass, Darkly

*Who is she, this girl who, standing toe to heel with the one before her moves into view with opacity? Shadow girl she is, like the rest, but she is clear — clearer than any who have stepped forth before. She is the "me" with whom my dark side identifies; she is the "me" who searched the universe for fame but found only tattered dreams and imaginary friendships. She is the "me" who sought self-hood in others, only to find that others could not reflect the light.*

*Without the light, she remains unseen, a shadow, Peter Pan in drag. Wishing to become Tinkerbell, the shadow-girl was naught but the spectre of unresolved fears, unbidden hardship, and unrequited love. Not even would she resemble Wendy, for shadow-girl could not grow up. She could not overcome her fears. Before the mirror now, I can see her peering at me with clear eyes; sad eyes; lonely eyes*

*I remember her, dead to rights; I remember the dreams behind those eyes; I remember the tears shed over the heart that resides on the shadow-girl's sleeve. Look at me! Shadow-girl! Do you remember me? Seeking fame and fortune, we found neither. Seeking love and laughter, well…it's a temporary happiness, but for a while we could pretend it was real. Once in a while, it seemed it might be so.*

### Woman

1.
Lonely woman watches
Willows weep
Then ---
Falls asleep

2.
Lonely lady laughs,
Longng,
Little sister cries

3.
Dancing daughters die
Daily –
Becoming someone new

4.
Wise woman watches
Closely
Man's face soon changes

5.
The bird on the branch
Knows my anguish
Her song calls
Her own despair

© *August 1993*

# Chapter 15: Beachmare

Phoenix was so immersed in her lifestyle that she had no idea that the dark depth of her rock and roll dream was simply a sucking whirlpool created by her actions. Phoenix was a statistic, a young woman taken advantage of in the military, an abused spouse who was so affected by her experience that all relationships since had been continuations of abuse in one form or another. Now that she was not in a relationship, Phoenix spent more time with Lavender at nightclubs, dancing or banging heads to one band or another.

It was a late spring day when they went early to a club and found the headlining band in the middle of their sound check. This out-of-town band was good and the musicians were fun. The girls were giddy when they were asked to oversee product sales during that night's show. They were tasked with organizing tapes, t-shirts, and bumper stickers on a table, selling them, as well as collecting names for a mailing list. This was exactly the kind of thing the two rock-n-roll women loved to do. It made them feel important and wanted. It gave them purpose.

These days, Phoenix and Lavender drew attention wherever they went, for they spent hours creating their own unique clothing and makeup styles that could hardly be considered conformist. Thrift store prom dresses encountered the pinking shears to become rag-doll chic. They painted their faces with bright colors, flowers and birds drawn with eyeliner, and dotted rainbows made of eye shadow. There were times when, as they walked down the street from home to club, plastic cups filled with alcohol and cola, a stranger would stop the girls and ask for photographs.

Truly, they never knew if these tourists with cameras thought the girls were so strange-looking they had to have a photo, or if they thought they'd stumbled upon a couple of wayward rock stars. After all, once in a while a child would stop Phoenix in the street and ask if she was a famous singer, Cyndi

Lauper. She would chuckle as she denied that Ms. Lauper was likely to be walking down these streets, moving past the children into the evening.

This night, they were at their second-hand best. The band they had come to see came from the west coast. The west coast, they said, was the place for Phoenix and her friend. Not here, in this conservative city, so far from the real action of rock and roll. So many people told the girls this over the span of the evening that they decided it just might be true. They began to make plans. They put those plans into action within days.

Phoenix and Lavender made a preliminary vacation trip to Los Angeles, though it could not rightfully be called a "vacation." Taking with them only the clothing they could wear and as much cheap costume jewelry as possible, Phoenix and Lavender hit the road. Hitchhiking together had proven safe in the past, and without any money, it seemed a good way to travel. They created alter-personas, took on different names, and made up their histories on the fly as they spoke with the hapless individuals who offered rides. They made it across their own city in two rides. The second man who picked them up promised he would take them as far as the westernmost exit to the freeway. Only, he said he wanted to first stop at his apartment along the way to pick up some gas money and call his employer.

The girls looked at one another with pursed lips and discussed it quietly. Both thought it might not be a good idea, but decided to agree to this plan. They would have waited for him in the car, but the man seemed benign, so they accompanied him into his apartment, walking past small gatherings of unemployed apartment dwellers drinking beer in the mid-afternoon. As Phoenix and Lavender waited in the man's living room, they heard him talking on the phone. After he hung up, it seemed to take longer than necessary for him to return to the living room. Something seemed off. Phoenix and

Lavender glanced at one another, silently communicating that perhaps it would be a good idea to get out of there fast.

The two women were just about ready to leave when the man came back into the living room — stark naked! The women moved in unison, headed for the door. The man ran across the room, pushing them aside and planting himself in front of the door. Undaunted, Phoenix and Lavender forced their way to the door, and yanked it open. As they ran toward the freeway, they could hear the laughter of the neighbors as the wide-thrown door revealed the man's folly.

It was to be the only potentially dangerous moment in the girls' "vacation." They arrived in a city just south of Los Angeles two long semi-truck rides later, and walked as far as the beach to find the apartment where Lavender's mother lived with her husband. After a short visit, they drove the girls to Los Angeles, where they left them at the apartment of some friends of Lavender's who had recently moved from the city where the women currently lived.

Phoenix and Lavender stayed a few days, discovering Venice Beach and Hollywood. On Sunset Strip, Phoenix found that she could pass for much younger than her age of almost-thirty. They made new friends among the young people who hung around the rock clubs along the Strip. both women felt they had found their magical home. Making plans to return as soon as they could, they took their thumbs back to the highway. They arrived without mishap at the apartment and prepared to pack up and move.

Neither Phoenix nor her friend had been gainfully employed for a couple of months, and *avante-garde* as they were, finding paying jobs was unlikely in their city. They were living in an apartment vacated by the young gay couple whose apartment they had stayed in while they visited Los Angeles. By the time they decided to move, daily fare consisted of ketchup packages swiped from fast-food joints spread on day-old bread or mixed in water like soup.

It wasn't difficult for the women to pack up what little they owned and put it in storage. They carried with them only what they could wear or toss in backpacks. Phoenix took with her only her poetry and both women wore every earring they owned in their multiple ear piercings.

Phoenix's old boyfriend, the gentle and kind bass player, with whom she had remained friends as she had hoped, put the girls' belongings in storage and bought them bus tickets to Los Angeles. Their story about the naked man clinched his resolve to help them remain as safe as possible in their adventure. The girls returned to California in relative luxury in the middle of the night. When they arrived at the bus station, Phoenix contacted an aunt and uncle who lived in the Los Angeles area, hoping to procure a ride from the station. Unfortunately, she was not aware enough to realize the imposition she would be making simply by making the phone call. Her aunt groggily told her they lived too far away to help. Phoenix felt stupid for making the call. Lavender called her mother, who lived further away. She and her husband came to the station and delivered the girls to Venice Beach. Phoenix and Lavender moved in with their friends, the previous tenants of the apartment they had just vacated.

It was a very small apartment, consisting of just one large room, a closet-sized kitchen, and a mid-sized bathroom. Situated just one block from Venice Beach, the apartment seemed to be owned by the cockroaches. Nevertheless, there was a romantic mystique about the place, for long-time local residents told them that poet and singer Jim Morrison had spent many a night on the roof in the distant 1960s past. Such a poetic story did not mean as much to Lavender, but for Phoenix this was exciting.

For a short while the women and their friends shared the large room, placing a wall divider in the center of the room. Phoenix and Lavender found day jobs at Venice Beach restaurants, and began to live a much more adventurous life than even they could have imagined. After a few weeks,

Phoenix had changed jobs, now working at the same café where Lavender worked. They were paid cash on a daily basis. Each day, they would take their pay and head directly to the liquor store across the knoll from their apartment where they would purchase alcohol and mixers, then head back to the apartment where they would spend an hour creating their unique Hollywood heavy metal/punk-girl personas.

Carrying huge drinks they had mixed in covered plastic cups procured at the convenience store, they would head to the bus stop and Sunset Strip. Ostensibly, the girls were working toward starting a rock promotion business. In their hearts, they were still searching for true love. In reality, they were searching for themselves.

## Dark Dungeon

In the darktime
There is loneliness;
The quiet ticking
Of the clock
Is the beat of the heart
That lies not beside;
Reminder of betrayals,
Of love once believed
The soft hum of electric things
Has become night's companion
Silence would be perhaps a blessing
Yet perhaps a curse; for then
The lonely darktime
Would close in
Like dungeon walls
And chain the emptiness
Forever in the night

© *22 November 1996*

**Broken Promises**

Undoubtedly young people
Will whimper when
Reminded of lifetimes
Of promises profoundly
Given, and
Greedily taken away;
Why winsome minds
Should seduce suicide
As though it were a
Warm winter wrap
Pulled tight around
A cold lonely heart
Is more than a question,
For there can be no answer
And yet, in my empty
Locker lies lonely
DEATH: Deep shed tears
Will wash away none
Of the blood that beats
Furious, river rapid
Anger each time
I, too, am reminded
Of lifetimes of promises
Broken, and of
Loneliness.

*(c) 10 May 1987*

**Space-Time**

Life is a succession of
Missed opportunities
And mistaken identities
It's a wistful moment
When we pass through a
Rift in the continuum
And recognize a soul
Who does not know us

The tears are meant
To cleanse our souls
And leave us hopeful
We must not, like Alice,
Drown in our tears, but
Move on to the next
Opportunity, dry eyed and
Stronger for our knowledge

That each time we chance
The meeting of souls, we
Come closer to touching
One who is also
Reaching out for us – and
Along the way, do we not
Chance upon new friends
And old souls we have
All but forgotten,
Embracing them to our
Ever-expanding heart?

© *24 April 2000*

## Interim 4: The Scrying Mirror

*The mirror reflects a myriad of me's. Superimposed like a chain of paper-dolls, one after the other they stand, reminding me of why I am who I am. Each a little different, each a little stronger than the one before, the mirror-me's accuse me of my failure to rise. Phoenix has not risen from the ashes, in spite of attempts and momentary morphological mistakes. One night with a rock star or a few months on Sunset Strip does not make Phoenix a music promoter, or anything more than a woman of poor choices and shattered dreams.*

*The morphing mirror-me's replay times that came between then and now, times that must be remembered before the shadow-girl might really reach out to me and silently disappear. But the time to remember them is not yet, for the tether is still tied, hiding beneath the disguises the mirror girls reflect.*

*Which am I?*

*Who am I?*

## Chamomile Dreams

Dreams in chamomile,
Drapes of lace
Old woman's tea cups
Cracked, and placed
Amongst old poetry,
Portraits and songs
Of chamomile dreams
And hand-made lace

In chamomile dreams
And rocking chair
She weaves yet spells
For others' fare
She sighs for love
She'd had and lost
She cries for her
Loneliness – the cost
Of dreams of chamomile
And lace

She thinks of the young girl
She once had been
And the beautiful boys;
The kind-hearted men
Destined, like treasure
To slip through her hands

Diamonds scattered
Upon her place
Of chamomile dreams
And worn-out lace.

© *21 May 1995*

## Chapter 16: From the Ashes...

It's been many years now since Phoenix left the rock-n-roll lifestyle in pursuit of a sense of constancy and commitment. One day as they wandered the boardwalk at Venice Beach planning a party at their apartment, she and Lavender spied a young man leaning against the counter of a pizza joint. Phoenix thought he was good looking and said so to Lavender. After a bit of discussion, they invited him to the party. They never expected many of those they invited to actually attend their events, but they asked people to come anyway. This time, the young man and a few of his friends joined the girls and their motley handful of friends. Squeezing into the small apartment, attendees reveled in loud music and alcohol.

Phoenix and the young man seemed to connect, and soon after the party they began to see one another. The couple lasted for a while until one day they simply went their separate ways. The young man sometimes made jokes that Phoenix didn't find at all funny. The jokes and comments poked fun at other people, particularly those who were of different backgrounds.

He once threatened another young man whom Phoenix had befriended well before she came upon him leaning like James Dean against the pizza shop's front counter. When Phoenix asked him about his comments, he convinced her that he had only been joking. In her loneliness, she had felt what she thought was love when she was with him, and when he told her he loved her, she chose to believe him. However, the two had not make any commitment to one another, and when he stopped coming by to visit, Phoenix took it in stride. Phoenix and Lavender were to remain in the apartment for a while longer, but the young man soon disappeared from the beach.

Not long after Phoenix and the young man stopped seeing one another, she discovered that she was soon to be a mother once again. She had not taken precautions, for she secretly desired a child. She felt such a heavy burden after losing her daughter so long ago. The guilt haunted her in the quiet moments. Her broken heart yearned for an opportunity to love and protect a child as she had not been able to with the Princess. She had been a terrible mother, unable to protect her child from the abuse. Now, Phoenix felt a strange mixture of fear and joy that she had been given another chance. She felt that she could give this child a better life than she had been able to offer the Princess of her youth.

Phoenix moved from the big California city to the place where her family was living. It was here that she bore her Jasmine. This daughter had been conceived upon the very roof that had once been the sleeping place of Jim Morrison. Forgetting the little hints of cruelty and prejudice she and Lavender had heard the young man utter, Phoenix was sure that her newborn daughter had been conceived in love. Her overactive imagination built a romantic story around the short assignation she had with the young man at Venice Beach. Now that he was but a memory, the relationship became a mystical experience in which Phoenix's dream of motherhood came true. Their story became a fairytale in which Phoenix was the princess waiting for her prince.

Inexplicably, though she did not yet truly trust men in the area of long-term relationships, and in spite of the pure happiness she felt at having her beautiful Jasmine Flower in her life, Phoenix still yearned to be part of a couple. She decided she *must* have truly loved the Jasmine Flower's father and that he had loved her. They had been separated by circumstances. She began a search for him to tell him that they had a daughter together. Certainly, she felt that if nothing else, he had a right to know that he had a child.

### Sweet, He Left

I touch my fingers
To the sea,
And foam sprytes gather all
'round me
I pass my hand
O'er all the land
Time shifts thoughts
Like whispering sand
I sit upon a dark,
Damp stone
Think still my heart
Beats quite alone
Waves rush in my
Quiet ear
From empty eye
Falls one still tear
For sprytes have left;
I watched them go;
Dark crystal depths
Are all I know
I had a love;
I held his hand
We left our
Prints upon the sand
Then, like the winds
That scream and moan
I turned:
And left him
All alone.
And he unknowing,
Left a flower.
Sweet, he left
A jasmine flower!

© *12 July 1988*

Using telephone books for information, she wrote letters to people in the metropolitan area where he had told her he was from. If they had the same last name as his, they received a letter from Phoenix. She asked them if they happened to know him, and if they did, to please pass on the information that she was trying to locate him with some news. She didn't share the news with them, because she wanted the opportunity to tell him herself either in a direct letter or on the telephone.

When Jasmine Flower was three years old, Phoenix found the child's father. One of her letters had arrived in his aunt's mailbox, and she reached out to him. He called Phoenix at the telephone number she had provided in the letter. They spoke on the phone for some time. He had returned to his hometown, just as she had suspected. During that first conversation, Phoenix had a sign that the "jokes" he had made while at Venice Beach were a true indication of who he was, but she was oblivious to the implications at the time.

The person he had become in her imagination overpowered the reality. After a few conversations, he decided he would like to move to where Phoenix lived and meet their daughter. They married soon after he arrived. As usual, Phoenix was convinced that this was the husband of her destiny. Within a year, Phoenix had given birth to another girl, her beloved Addie, whose quiet demeanor would belie her later strength and commitment to a meaningful life.

Once again, the old adage "hindsight is 20/20" was proven correct. Phoenix soon discovered the truth. This man whom she had married was a criminal, a drug addict; and a neo-Nazi with a record of violence. During their short time as a married couple, he revealed that in spite of his decision to marry her, he was not really attracted to Phoenix. He had even written in a letter to his mother that she was not "the best-looking girl" he could find, though she was "a good woman." His mother shared this letter with Phoenix, somehow thinking this would convince her that he was worth waiting for. Her daughters' father went to jail for a variety of crimes that Phoenix had been oblivious about.

As she reviewed their time together, a number of his comments and behaviors began to glow like neon in her mind. She recalled how she would lie awake in the middle of the night wondering where he was, not knowing he was out committing crimes against people she knew.

### 3 a.m.

In the noise that is meant
To be the Silence of the night
I hear the screams…
The screams of my heart
Beating loneliness…Loneliness? Why?
It should be wrapped in the sounds
Of the blanket of dark'
Held tight in the arms that profess
Love and protection.
The emptiness of the night is thick:
A cacophony, flowing cold like
The slowness of a river in winter,
Black honey, not sweet whippoorwill
Love night: but empty
I hear layers of life that is not mine
And a train that cuts through, a
Reminder that my loneliness is not
All that is; there is more
But I wait; and the space that has
Passed is four and a half times
The space that was promised; and I
Like in the dark as the river of night
Flows cold and wet, and lonely like
Death and I wonder why I cannot stop
My screams – the screams
Of my heart, and my unwanted loneliness

© *15 November 1991*

She remembered the baseball bat he pounded nails into and kept near their front door in spite of her protests. After he had his mother mail her a copy of a newspaper article in which he was apparently proud to be quoted, she remembered that one of the first questions he had asked her when they reconnected on the telephone was, "Are you Jewish?" In the newspaper article, he was recorded as yelling racist epithets at a black political candidate in his city.

She thought about how while she was at work thinking he was at his own workplace he had traded the meat out of their freezer and new clothing she had bought for the trip to the hospital to give birth to their second daughter for drugs. Begging her to help him, he had let her drive him to rehab before she left with the little ones for a visit with her parents. He was released from rehab after 72 hours. While she was out of town, he sold her beloved books and jewelry for the little bit of money they could bring to supply himself with drugs.

Though the drugs were a part of his life and possibly the purpose for his criminal activity, he had no drug charges against him. His many arrests were related to theft, assault, and arson. Later Phoenix would find out that the word "aggravated" had been attached to the assault and the arson charges. She couldn't help but wonder how she had not realized who she had married.

Belatedly, Phoenix learned that he had surreptitiously terrorized their now four-year-old daughter Jasmine. Phoenix was devastated. How could she miss such thing? How could "love" blind her so? While her husband served his time, Phoenix filed for divorce and worked toward severing all ties between him and her little family. All she wanted to do now was keep her daughters safe.

Sometime after this experience, Phoenix flashed back on the moment after her drunken poetic-punk lover cut open her hand. She recalled the moment when, as she underwent stitches, the doctor told her that it might behoove her to look for a pattern in her relationships. At the time, she had dismissed the idea. Her parents had an excellent marriage and were still in love after all their years together. Phoenix had no frame of reference for the kind of marriage she had experienced. It was an anomaly. Not realizing how her first marriage itself had been a choice driven by the damage inflicted upon her while in the Air Force, she compartmentalized her relationships as if they were separate and unrelated. She had begun to think that maybe she was broken. She considered leaving behind all thought of men and marriage, throwing herself into raising her daughters, working, growing her spirituality, and honing her writing skills. For a time, she did just that.

### Holy Ground

I dance upon the ground
Left Holy by children
Who played doll's house
And jacks beneath a searing sun
Cool moon lets light drops
Refresh my mourning mind;
No more shall I remain alone.
On Holy ground,
This daughter stands
Palms upturned to Mother Love
What shall I dance?
Shall it be Sistersong
Or Hermit's Repose upon
Sand beat flat
By little rainbow feet?
Open armed, I reach for
Mother Love, and find
Bright my heart
Which once
Had known the Dark

© *24 April 1991*

When Addie was three and a half years old, Phoenix had become involved once more in public poetry readings. It was during this time period that she ran across her "blood-brother," he of the crimson t-shirt and self-centered male-poet angst. Stricken by a physical chemical reaction that was still surprisingly strong after all those years, Phoenix almost slipped into the weird world of the night people once more. Teetering on the edge of that powerful drive, she pulled herself up and out before she fell in.

Her beloved girls were her lifeline. With them at home and counting on her for everything, she knew a fall into that darkness was out of the question. It was then that she remembered that she was strong enough to stand on her own. By now, she thought she might be ready for a relationship with someone. She didn't go out looking for someone, of course. Phoenix continued spending her free time writing and hanging out with her two girlfriends and their children.

It happened rather by accident. A few years before, when Phoenix was in the process of divorcing the father of her daughters, she had published a few poems and stories in a local metaphysical magazine. In fact, she had gotten one of little Jasmine's spoken-word pieces, which she had recorded as the precocious child made it up, published as well. In the course of business, Phoenix had spent some time in conversation with the editor and publisher, who was a married father of four. For the most part, they had talked about the technical aspects of the publications. However, sometimes their conversations turned to the subject matter. As such, they bent toward the spiritual and were always interesting.

When Phoenix was invited to be the featured reader at a poetry reading, she compiled a list of people she wanted to invite. She mailed invitations to old friends, keepers of metaphysical shops, and other people she had dealt with over the past few years. She decided it might be prudent to invite the magazine publisher and his spouse, as well as any staff they worked with, to the reading. When the day of the reading came and went without a word from anyone at the publication, she thought little of it, figuring they were simply not interested.

The reading went well, for the most part. Standing on stage reading a collection of her works was a little frightening, for this was the first opportunity she had to be the featured reader since her days at the art gallery. Phoenix invited one of her single-mom friends along to the reading. Her child was a teenager, old enough to be left home, while Phoenix hired a babysitter. It was the friend's idea to bring along a cooler full of beer, which they stowed in the trunk of Phoenix's car.

As Phoenix's nervousness mounted, she drank a beer before going in to the reading. It eased her fear a bit, and she spoke well enough. Only one minor "hiccup" occurred when, about half way through a longer, rather sensual piece, she looked up from her page and found herself staring straight into the eyes of a rather grandmotherly type of woman. In the moment, Phoenix forgot that age is no indication of personality, and she judged the woman as prim and proper with lightning speed. A sudden wave of embarrassment ran through her body, causing her to hesitate. Fortunately, she returned to the work, finishing the piece without further trouble.

In the end, the only part of the evening which still causes Phoenix consternation is the moment just after she left the stage. In the exhilaration of having completed the reading, she rushed to the door, heading to the car where her friend sat with a beer in hand. On the way out the door, a young man stopped her, saying, "thank you." Her mind on escape, Phoenix blurted out, "For what?" before scuttling past him. When he answered, "well, for the reading, of course," she flushed in humiliation and virtually ran to the car. Where her friend waited with a cold beer in hand.

Phoenix still wonders, years later, if the man had been one of the old friends she had invited, whom she had not seen for a very long time. Once in a while she even ponders the possibility that it was someone from one of the publications that she had mailed invitations to, or even the owner of a venue who might have been worth getting to know.

Two weeks after the reading, a letter from the publisher of the small metaphysical magazine arrived in her mailbox. In the letter, he thanked her for her invitation, and wrote that the magazine had folded. He and his wife, who was his partner in the venture, had parted ways. That initial correspondence led to more letters, some phone calls, and eventually a dinner date. From their previous conversations, Phoenix and the publisher knew they had much in common. Over time, they entered into a relationship based on common interests, respect, and a friendship that had begun with those first conversations about Phoenix's submissions to the magazine.\

Unfortunately, neither individual was yet ready for a new relationship. Neither had thought through the decision they made to get together, though the publisher did attempt to tell Phoenix that he was "not in a good place" for entering a serious relationship. Phoenix, ever the daydreamer, imagined that they had enough in common to overcome any bumps. She was not in love with the publisher, but she cared about him, and felt that between the two of them and their children, they could make a family.

In reality, it can take a long time to recover from the trauma of a broken relationship, whether there has been abuse or not. Phoenix had been divorced from her second husband for about three years at the time she and the publisher began to live together. The publisher's divorce was still fresh and the relationship unresolved. After they had been together for five months, Phoenix chose to walk away. By then, she was expecting another child. Seven months later, she gave birth to her son, a strapping lad she called Evan. It was years before Evan's father forgave Phoenix for leaving. Perhaps he never fully has, though the time has come that their friendship has rekindled and Evan spends time with his father and the siblings on his paternal side.

**Labor**
Within
    A poem
        Belly deep…
           Pregnant words.
         Burst forth:
       The product
Of desire.

*© 5 January 1995*

# Interim 5: Dark Moon

*When will the shadow wraith let me go, and let me know which, if any, I am? In full daylight, the mirror reflects only myself as I am today, standing beside my daughters and my son, whose ancient eyes hold secrets to a future the shadow-girl will never know.*

*Because of her, I cannot understand the promise they send, for the tether about my ankles holds me back. Because of her, I find myself standing once more, in the shadows, gazing into a mirror, darkly, remembering her, and the next girl, and the next. Because of her, the girls in disguise remind me of lovers who have never been the true love, the one love, destined to fulfill a promise of bright blessings beyond the flames from which Phoenix must arise.*

*Outside, there is no moon, as I stand central to the glass, and watch as the other girls, the tethered chain-gang, step into motion and show me their part in the pile of ashes that lie at my feet. I watch, and I wait, for the times to tell their stories have yet to come. I will wait.*

*What else can I do?*

## Chapter 17: Forgiveness

When Evan was about two years old, and Phoenix and her children were living with a friend and her children. Phoenix had been in pain from what had been initially diagnosed as rheumatoid arthritis for months. She had taken harsh medications for RA for two years before getting pregnant with Evan. Recently, however, she had been told it had been a misdiagnosis. It was now identified as fibromyalgia. She had almost crippling pain and had used a cane throughout most of her pregnancy. She had fallen prey to the depression and inability to cope which often accompanies chronic pain. She had left another government job and was not working outside the home. Now she cared for the home and her friend's children as well as her own. In this way, she earned her keep and her friend saved the money she would have spent on child care.

Phoenix was struggling with her spirituality and searching for a place she could call her metaphysical home. She had prayed in many different ways for health and for love for a long time. Following family tradition, all the children were baptized as infants in mainstream Protestant denominations. Phoenix had attended Methodist, Lutheran, Unitarian, and Unity churches, as well as Wiccan and Pagan gatherings off and on for many years. She and her friend were active in the local Pagan community. Phoenix wrote and distributed a small metaphysical newsletter and created inspired Goddess-oriented artworks, some of which were on sale at a local occult book and gift shop. Still she felt there was something else she needed to understand about her spirituality.

It was in the midst of this spiritual melee that Phoenix had what she would later refer to as a Wesleyan "warming of the heart" that assured her that the Holy was active in her life and that she could forgive. It happened in the strangest place. The children were all down for a nap, and Phoenix was simply walking through her friend's kitchen, considering what to cook for dinner.

All of a sudden, between deciding whether to cook pork chops or hamburgers, Phoenix was compelled to stop — stock-still — in the center of the room. She felt as if something had opened up above her like a skylight. She knew in an instant that she was forgiven for her poor choices, for her inability to protect her child, and for everything she had ever done and would ever do. More importantly, like a flash of lightning that ran through her in the very same moment that she forgave herself, she forgave her first husband for the abuse.

All of her anger at him was gone. Phoenix didn't forget what she had been through. This experience didn't suddenly erase the experiences from her life. She simply seemed to let go of the garbage the experiences had piled on her — in her mind and in her heart, in her soul and in her life. It happened so fast, and with such fervor that she was aghast that it even crossed her mind. She had not been thinking about any of that in the moments before this experience. She was considering what to make for dinner that night with no thought of her past or her future, of her enemies or her friends. The feeling was so intense that even as she thinks of it today, she can picture herself standing there, full of a light that was inexplicably bright and inexplicably warm.

She did know yet that there was more to the story. She didn't yet realize that she had been raped twice while in the Air Force. She didn't know that those experiences, hidden deep within, had led her into the darkness of abuse. She also didn't know that though she seemed to let the baggage go, she had in reality simply put it away. She hid it in a dark inner closet where she couldn't see it so she could move on. When she later began to explore that closet, she would find that she had unknowingly judged herself guilty of the crimes that had been perpetrated upon her. She had forgiven herself for making mistakes, but it would take many more years before she could forgive herself for the judgement which she had executed upon herself.

## New In You

I feel that in You
I am new
At a depth
Few have known
Like the sand
Made new by
The swift running stream
Like the soil newly turned
Or a fresh drop of dew
A full clear tone
Rung from a bell tower
Heard across town
Or the dance of a wind
That kisses the face
With a memory of love
Sent to the skies
A millennium ago…
You, Who knows my ever-breaking
Heart have touched my tears
And warmed them to diamonds
You have left on my heart
The promise of something
That will come when my soul
Is truly new

©9 June 2008

## Chapter 18: New Life

Phoenix had forgiven herself for the mistakes she had made, but her life didn't turn around immediately. Throughout her life, as arbitrary and foolish as her choices had been, Phoenix had known that there was something more. She had always sensed that there was Something greater, Something which somehow held her together in spite of herself. This Divine Something connected everything and everyone; of this Phoenix felt perfectly sure.

She had felt this as a young child, and as a preteen she used to take solitary walks to talk to God. Whether her family lived in the Arizona desert or the Michigan woods, Phoenix's treks into nature lovingly carrying her diary, a pen, and a book were as a life-blood to her. As a nine-year-old, hovering over her brothers and sisters in the family living room while her body lay in a hospital bed in a burn ward convinced her even then that there was more to the world than her eyes could see.

Perhaps as a result of her early premonition about the fire and subsequent out-of-body-experience, when Phoenix was young, she became interested in the world of unexplained phenomena and the unseen. By the time she was twelve, she was reading everything she could find about the subject. She read every book she came across by "ghost hunter" Hans Holzer, Sybil Leek's *Diary of a Witch*, and various books and stories about mediums and true hauntings beginning when she was in sixth grade. As she grew into adulthood, she began to experiment with different spiritual paths, searching for meaning. Somehow, she believed, her early awareness of a Divine connection was more than her imagination. The God she felt was real and immanent was much more than the God she had learned about in her intermittent Sunday School and Vacation Bible School classes at Methodist, Presbyterian, and Lutheran churches.

When she was seventeen, Phoenix was introduced to esoteric metaphysical practices by her first love — the

"Heathcliff" of her teen years and later rock-n-roll life. He had been her partner and mentor in a study of the *Kabbalah*, spiritualism, astrology, and what was then termed "the Craft.". The spiritual connection she felt as a child was enhanced by sharing the experience with others who were as curious as she was about the unseen and the unexplained. As part of her studies she had read various esoteric books, including a detailed reading of the King James Version of the Bible from the beginning to the end.

During her tumultuous first marriage, Phoenix sought solace in the Protestant church of her upbringing. Though she felt the Divine Presence in the beauty of the spaces where the people gathered to worship and in the kindness of one or two of those she met there, for the most part she felt judged and unwelcome in these Christian churches. Eventually she gave up trying to attend worship and classes. Instead, Phoenix took various free correspondence courses offered by certain denominations and religious groups, such as the Seventh Day Adventists and the Campus Crusade for Christ.

She looked at the library shelves and discovered many spiritual titles which had been popular among the young adults of the late 1960s and the 1970s. These fascinated her, and she dove headlong into a reading list that included Carlos Casteneda's *Teachings of Don Juan* series, *Siddhartha*, and *Zen and the Art of Motorcycle Maintenance*. She was hungry for knowledge and voraciously read whatever she could about spirituality, from Catholicism to Zen Buddhism.

Eventually her interest in all things spiritual combined with her negative experiences with men led her to discover the concept of the feminine Divine. Along with other women and men who felt they had somehow been hurt or felt rejected by their churches, she swayed on a pendulum away from the patriarchal religion that pervaded western society. In spite of her painful experiences, Phoenix did not hate men, but she had become a feminist in both her spirituality and in her mundane life.

When Jasmine was very small, Phoenix discovered a strong, active movement in feminist spirituality. Much of what she read in this area was similar to her earlier studies in the Craft, with more of a focus on earth religions of the ancient past and less on Judeo-Christian Mysticism. As Phoenix became more involved in this Wiccan practice and the Neo-Pagan community, the stronger and more centered she felt. This was something she needed as she still sought strength and empowerment after her first marriage.

Jumping in with both feet, Phoenix immersed herself in her new metaphysical studies. In this new spirituality, Phoenix discovered that she had an inner strength that she may not have recognized without spending time among Goddess-people and earth-religions. She honed her gift of writing by penning poetry and rites, as well as newsletter articles and other informational pieces. Later in life, it would become clear to Phoenix how important this experience was in her development, both as a woman and as a spiritual being.

### Drawing Down the Moon

Alone, I am
Mother-Woman-Child
My heart, like the
Phases of the Moon
I love so much
Wanes: then waxes...
Wanes: I am lonely.
The moon has a face
Like Mother Love –
Distant, beautiful, cold
Yet warm when drawn
Down to the depths of the
Loneliest daughter's soul.

©*15 November 1995*

Along that path, Phoenix met many sincere seekers and experienced a type of interfaith dialogue that many will never know. In learning about ancient and post-modern world religions and coming to understand Reconstructionist Neo-Paganism, Phoenix found anecdotal evidence of something they all had in common. Her heart was sparked with a desire to discover that commonality. She was convinced that at the center of all spiritualities, there is one Truth. Phoenix made it her goal to find that Truth. Though she had grown up and taken her physical life to many places, her spirit had never left the path forged by the little girl carrying her journal into the forest. She knew deep within that the Divine Something was real and much, much greater than any one religious understanding could encompass.

There was a person who Phoenix had met years before when she was a child. After a while, Phoenix became aware that this person had walked with her through her ordeals. He had picked her up when she fell and clothed her in an armor of Light that she could not always see, but somehow, she knew he was wrapped about her, warming her body and soul. Through dreams, Phoenix was reminded that he was there for her, even though to some observers it seemed she had abandoned his way. Those who thought she had lost her way did so because they believed there was only one way. Many of them still do.

Having experienced the connecting power of the Spirit through other spiritual practices, Phoenix came to understand the teachings of Jesus from a different perspective from the one she was taught as a youngster in Sunday School. This new understanding of Jesus' teachings both simplified and complicated Phoenix's perception of Christianity. The depth of a relationship with the Divine cannot be put into mere human words. In accepting that she was a follower of the *teachings* of Jesus, Phoenix would open the doors to a new struggle, which pitted her awareness that all life is connected by Spirit and that all creation is part of one living Divine

Something against church teachings that Christianity is the only "true" expression of that Divine Something. Her experiences showed Phoenix that not only were there many ways of meeting the Divine, but that there were other ways of interpreting the sacred texts of the religious system she was raised to believe in.

Phoenix continued to struggle with her concept of the Divine and her path toward what she now referred to as "At-one-ment;" that is, a state of being at one with the Divine Something and All That Is. However, she would take a turn in her path that would find her attempting to push her vision of the Divine back into a socially acceptable box even while acknowledging that this was an impossible feat.

### The Forest

There is a place where I can go to find Him
A place where Christ can be my only Friend
I walk among the Pine Trees and the Birches
There I know that Love will never end
I walk along the waters in the valleys
I feel His touch in every breath of air
I gather ferns and flowers, Ah! What beauty…
They are but little things that show His care
When I cannot go walking through the forest
To see the Truth in every falling leaf
That's when my heart becomes my special garden
And God within me fills me with belief.

© *7 May 1984*

Even as she meandered along the spiral path of alternative spiritualities, Phoenix had spent time in the church. She attended worship periodically and even taught Sunday School and Vacation Bible School. Her children were baptized as infants, mainly because it was a tradition that Phoenix respected. When the children grew older, she took them to church so they could learn the story of Jesus in a group setting. Eventually, she returned to church, by way of a secretarial position.

She thought it was just a short stopover, a job to be taken until another, better position opened up. She could not have known that this new job would open the door to a new kind of education. All the while as she had gamboled with goddesses, she was really learning to stand on her own two female feet, gaining self-esteem and building personal emotional, physical, and spiritual strength. Now it was time for Phoenix to learn to walk again among the practitioners of her childhood religious tradition.

Phoenix found meaning in her spiritual life – an attachment to All That Is and to a community that she always felt running through her like a string, connecting her as though she were a pearl on a necklace made of ancestors and children, friends and lovers, memories and experiences, hopes and dreams; practices and prayers.

It has always been difficult for Phoenix to locate her spirituality in a specific tradition. Her early days discovering the Divine under the sun, moon, and stars are journal pages written in indelible ink upon her soul. They cannot be torn from her. Perhaps because of this, Phoenix found that her understanding of that ineffable Divine Something that many call God and of the teacher Jesus transcends the boundaries of established denominations. In fact, she has not been able to reconcile her experiences with the belief of others that there is only one way to be spiritual. She has spent countless hours and words considering the meaning of the acceptable canon of Christianity. After years of attempting to follow such a narrow path, she was surprised to learn that she is not alone.

Discovering that there are many others within the walls of the church who have experienced the Divine in surprising places has been an enlightening and empowering experience for Phoenix. She is only one small part of an ongoing mystical movement toward a transcendent understanding of God. She believes that she defies boundaries, that though she has tried to live and grow within the confines of a specific religious and denominational tradition, she cannot be kept within those constraints. *God* cannot be kept within those constraints.

Attending a seminary where she expected to learn to work within the language and experiences of Christianity to become an ordained pastor within a mainline denomination, Phoenix found that this was not to be. Shifting paradigms within an organization must have an impetus from within, with leaders who are established and consistently a part of the organization. Though Phoenix had grown up attending church in the denomination in question, her connection to the organization had not been continuous nor consistent. It was not a task for which she was equipped.

One of the intents of a seminary education is to *deconstruct* the believer so that they might *reconstruct* themselves through critical thinking and letting go of preconceived ideas about what it means to be a believer. Phoenix realized that she had already been deconstructed. As she has grown over the years of her education she has found, not a new construct of herself, but evidence of the Truths that she had discovered on her own.

Today Phoenix is an ordained priest in a small Interspiritual church that was founded by previous members of a handful of mainline denominations. The founders sought to be more inclusive and accepting of all individuals. They found God in a variety of practices and teachings outside of the Christian church. Like Phoenix, they discovered Truth in ancient practices that enhance their metaphysical experience. As such, they are able to minister to those who do not feel comfortable within the boundaries of traditional Christianity.

Phoenix stands poised with an open ear and an open heart, awaiting the next step in a call that she hopes is becoming clearer. She no longer lives with a continuous empty, unwanted feeling. She knows that true romantic love comes unexpected. She understands now that love is more than the chemical reactions and desire to be wanted that she felt when she was young and alone. In those days, Phoenix was lonely even when she was not alone; now she can be alone without feeling lonely. Her awareness is piqued and she can feel the Presence of Love in the most bereft of places. It is her hope that she is able to awaken others to that Love when they are in dark places.

### Lord, Lord

Lord; Lord
In supplication
I kneel before you –
I open up my arms,
Inviting Love
Lord; Lord
My worship
Lives within me
I bow my lowly head
Requesting faith
Enter in my Heart
I pray, My God
Move within my soul,
I ask each day
Lord; Lord
With You beside me
I can see it:
My Spirit's free
(I know you walk with me)

© *13 September 1984*

It would be easy for Phoenix to regret her past, to step away from it and forget her mistakes, or to mourn for time lost. It would be easy to do, but it would also be pointless. For Phoenix has discovered that from the ashes of her past she is able to rise to meet the needs of others. She has been gifted with the ability to find hope in the darkest of nights and friends in the midst of strangers.

She has raised three of the most amazing children, whose lives have been neither perfect nor privileged, but have neither been lacking in love nor opportunity for growth. Looking back on her life to date, Phoenix recalls that prayer, faith, and long talks with God brought her through a childhood and young adulthood that held the potential for abject loneliness. When she was in the dark, there was always a Light, beckoning her to follow.

Moving around the United States, always the new girl – living with visible burn scars that frightened other children – fearing rejection, Phoenix could have allowed herself to wallow in self-pity. Marrying an abuser, discovering too late that there are people in the world who hurt those they profess to love, Phoenix might have responded with emotional or even actual suicide. Having self-harmed when she was struggling through her darkest times, she might have accidentally become a casualty of her depression.

Leaving the initial marriage, never pursuing counseling and slipping into the party life, she could easily have fallen into the dark abyss that often swallows the night people. Always seeking someone who would love her, Phoenix could have brought a succession of men into the lives of her children, putting them at risk in her never-satisfied thirst for belonging. There is much about Phoenix's life that she could regret; instead, she chooses to find the gifts that have come out of her experience. All there is to regret, perhaps, is the loss of a child and the time wasted in not knowing how strong she really was.

**Regret**

When I was young
I was afraid
Boys were a mystery
But I, I knew myself
And I was sure that I was the
Ugliest, most undesirable, fattest
Person to ever walk the earth, all
Five foot, three inches
one hundred and ten pounds of me
and no boy would ever
ever want me
but oh, how I wanted one of them
I wanted to be loved and cherished
Forever and ever, so badly
That when the first one came along
Who declared his undying love
For me, in tears, I fell head
Over heels, heels over head, and
Straight into the bed
Of terror
Oh, it took a couple of months
After wedding bells
For him to destroy what little self
Esteem I had, only a few months
To tear out my heart and my soul
And shove them into a closet
Where they cowered in fear
In those days there was no name
For that thing that I did with the
Wire cutters, the knives and the scissors
To my arms, but I
I knew that the only way to release
My fear, my frustration, my anger and
My … hope less ness
Was by rending my very flesh

Until the day
After eight years I gained the courage
To rescue my heart and my soul
And walk away
I have no regrets about those years,
For me…you see,
Today, this day, I know who I am
I know I am beautiful; I know I am sensual,
I know my strength and my power and
My control over my future
And I also know that girl
That girl, who at 15, 16, 17, 18…25
Did not know who she was
Did not know she had power
Did not know she was beautiful
I know her, and I know her loneliness
I know her fears and I recall her tears
For her, I have regret
I regret the loss
Of her innocence, the loss of her dreams
And the loss of her years
To the legacy of tears
For these things…
For these things,
I have regret.

© *15 September 2010*

Phoenix is able to look back at those years knowing that it is nothing short of a miracle that she lived through the 1970s as a teen without becoming addicted to drugs; she survived the 1980s without contracting a sexually transmitted disease; she made it beyond the 1990s and into the twenty-first century without losing hope that one day she would know what it meant to love herself.

## I; Dorcas

I; Dorcas
(Having once been dead)
Found Life in Christ
He built it
High upon a rock
Cephas – Peter
Father of Your church
Reached out –
"Tabitha, Arise"
A whisper.
A calling.
I; Dorcas
Look up at strength
~ Sweet Simon~
Proclaiming to the Lord
Of my rebirth
I once was dead
(Believing; Unredeeming)
Until those words
Reached through me
Healing – Saving – Loving
"Tabitha, Arise)

© *30 May 1984*

In fact, Phoenix's life is proof that love comes in surprising ways in times least expected. Twenty years after meeting him, Phoenix has married the real love of her life. They had both been married at the time they met, and had been friends since that day and into the days after their marriages ended. In the hustle and bustle of daily living, they lost track of one another until a chance discovery on the internet brought them back into one another's worlds.

There is no doubt in Phoenix's mind that true romantic love exists, and that she has finally found it. There is no "knight in shining armor," no leading man singing at the door like in the musicals she watched with her mother as a child. There is no rock star. What there is, Phoenix has discovered, is a good man with a good heart and a deep spiritual connection that cannot be shaken. They have much in common; they understand one another, and when things don't seem to be going quite the way they had hoped, they both know that the world will not end.

Both Phoenix and her husband believe that as they have made it through the lives they have had and the choices they have made, they will forge through whatever else may come with the strength of Spirit. They have a shared vision for their lives, each pursuing the artistic gifts they were born with and a deeper connection to All That Is, and to one another. They support one another in their pursuits, and work together to make their home a place of comfort. No day goes by without one or the other of them reminding the other how thankful they are that they found one another. If there is any regret between them, it is that they did not come together earlier in their lives.

Phoenix continues to try to better follow the teaching of Jesus to help "the least, the last, and the lost," and to "…love the Lord your God with all your heart and with all your soul and with all your strength and with all your mind and your neighbor as yourself." (Luke 10:27, NRSV). She practices prayer and meditation to center herself each day, and when she notices herself losing that center, she does whatever she can to regain it. With the knowledge of her years of different kinds of practice, Phoenix finds there is something available to her to strengthen in her time of need. She believes there is One Spirit, One Love, One Universe, expressed in the multivalent revelations of culture and experience.

# Interim 6: A New Kind of Glass

*After the fires of passion, comes a smoldering pleasantness reminiscent of tender times and hopes that once seemed possible. There is no reason to allow the smoldering embers to die, for they are but the incense of a life fully lived, whether it be well lived or naught. From these ashes, these memories still warm and newly stirred, comes the Phoenix: she is like the Amazon Princess of old; no mewling girl-child curled in the corner awaiting some faerie-tale prince to save her from herself.*

*She has been that Princess before; two-dimensional, like a paper-doll cut from an old catalogue, pasted together with the dreams of others. It was that paper princess who, tossed by the wayward winds, got lost for a while and almost drowned in the gutter, sucked into the depths of near despair and hopelessness. There was no reason for her loss of self; only that she allowed herself to be tossed upon the waves of societal expectations, finding excuses for letting others claim her shadow-selves, never allowing them to become more than a series of stories connected by the unseen chain of hope and unexpected selfhood.*

*I stand today before the glass, and it is no longer the mirror that taunted me with the reflections of my shadow-selves. Today, it is a window: clear, spotless, and faultless. Oh, still there is a reflection; the window is glass, after all. The shadow-selves are no longer visible; there is no chain holding me fast, link by link, to the many me's that were my past. No, today I know that the shadow-selves are within me; I have become one with myself and the chain has transformed into something better, something brighter. Before, the chain seemed to hold me fast with those shadow-girls; sallow, sad, lonely, bulimic, and afraid.*

*Today, the chain surrounds me like a bright armor of hard-forged chain-mail. It is my aura, my protection against a world that would have me be less than who I was made to be in the first place. It is my halo, my bright and shining Light of Love given me by the Universe that I might recognize myself and love myself and thus claim my right to walk along the path with Jesus. For now, I love myself so that I may love my neighbor as the Divine Something would have me do. No shadow-girl could do that.*

*In the window I can see myself reflected, fully whole yet expectant. It is a window now, for I no longer see only myself reflected, no longer see the shadow-girl cowering in the corner. In the window, I can see the world! It is a glorious, bright, and living world. It is my future and my children's future. It is the world in which I live so that I may carry my gift of hope to the other shadow-girls; to the shadow-boys — to the least, the last, and the lost. I stand before the window, gazing through my own reflection into the world and I begin to see the reflection of the Light of the World. I understand now that I am to be this reflection. I am to turn the mirrors of darkness into window; with the strength of Spirit I am to help the shadow-children to see themselves in the Light.*

*I open the window and step through — there is no longer a reflection of myself before me. This is the Phoenix: no longer am I dark dying shadows chained to sadness and death; I soar into this world alight with the rainbow of promise, clothed in the flames of a new Desire. All I can see now is the shining radiance of Love, lighting the world anew.*

## Chapter 19: Reunion

Many years after Phoenix lost her first child to Child Protective Services in a state that had only closed adoptions, she filed the paperwork to find her child in hopes of a reconciliation of sorts. By this time she had three more children and was temporarily fostering a niece. At that point in time, she was working at a big box store, working her way back into full time secretarial work and considering going back to school. The paperwork she sent in to CPS in the state where everything had taken place was returned to her with a note stating that she would have to wait until the child was at least twenty-one years old. There were still a couple years to go.

Year after year passed, and Phoenix thought about trying to connect again, but each time she thought about it, she became overwhelmed with fears about all the things that could go wrong. What if her Princess didn't want to know her? What if she actually hated her for what had happened, for being unable to protect her? For letting her go? As the years came and went, Phoenix was more and more afraid for what would happen if she met her daughter. She let the years slip by, focusing on the children she had, her parents and extended family, and her education.

Then one evening, when the children were grown and living on their own, she sat with her husband watching a television show and fiddling with her smartphone, checking social media. A message came in on one of the apps, a message which made her heart pound and her palms sweat with excitement. It was from her Princess! The very first message she received was *"I'm your Princess and I forgave you years ago for your mistakes. I'm here when you are ready."*

That very evening, they messaged back and forth for hours. Her firstborn daughter lived in another state only a day's drive away from her. In fact, the Princess had been visiting a close friend who lived within a ten-mile radius of Phoenix's home for many years. By the end of their online conversation, they had a plan to meet.

Two months later, Phoenix and her lost little Princess sat across from one another at a small restaurant getting to know each other. Since that time, they have gotten to know each other well. Phoenix and her husband were thrilled to meet Princess's husband, and as a bonus, Phoenix discovered her three grandsons – who in turn have met their cousins – Phoenix's four beautiful granddaughters! Princess and her half-siblings have become great friends.

After all the tears and heartache; after all the dark moments hiding in the shadows, Phoenix stands fully in the light, heart open with love and hope for the future.

*Phoenix and her Princess on the day the met anew*

## L(ove)

Beloved, I sing to You of Love
I join with You in the Light Love Shines
Upon my heart, O Beloved,
And, yes, upon the Hearts of all
Who love You
And whom You Love,
I give thanks, O Beloved
For the essence of All That Is
Woven into the Hearts of All
Peace

*© 1998, 2023*

## Y(outh)

Yea, I have sat beneath the
Mighty oak, O Beloved, and pondered the
Passing of Youth as the children
Enter new phases, like the moon
Darkens and brightens through the
Turning of the Year
Youth is Your touch as a
Blessing of Babes,
Yet as we grow Your touch is still the
Caress of parent to child, You are the
Sun in our passing year, and the moon
In our dark places of learning
Yea, O Divine, as I enter new phases, I
See diminishing youth as a journey to You
And still I feel Your touch as a
Blessing of the Ages.
May it be ever so

*© 1998, 2023*

In the circle
The women dance
Chanting, calling
Powers almost
Forgotten.
It has been
The mothers who
Have remembered,
Secretly.

©1 July 94

## Statistics*

- In the United States, an average of 20 people are physically abused by intimate partners every minute. This equates to more than 10 million abuse victims annually.
- 1 in 3 women and 1 in 4 men have been physically abused by an intimate partner.
- 1 in 5 women and 1 in 7 men have been severely physically abused by an intimate partner.
- 1 in 7 women and 1 in 18 men have been stalked. Stalking causes the target to fear she/he or someone close to her/him will be harmed or killed.
- On a typical day, domestic violence hotlines nationwide receive approximately 20,800 calls.
- The presence of a gun in a domestic violence situation increases the risk of homicide by 500%.
- Intimate partner violence accounts for 15% of all violent crime.
- Intimate partner violence is most common among women between the ages of 18-24.
- 19% of intimate partner violence involves a weapon.

*From the National Coalition Against Domestic Violence: http://www.ncadv.org/*

## Resources

- National Domestic Violence Hotline: 800-799-7233
- National Sexual Assault Hotline 800-656-HOPE (4673)
- National Suicide Prevention Hotline: 988
- Find a Domestic Violence Shelter in Your Area: https://www.domesticshelters.org
- National Coalition Against Domestic Violence: http://www.ncadv.org/
- WomensLaw.org  http://www.womenslaw.org/
- Centers for Disease Control Violence Prevention Data Sources: https://www.cdc.gov/violenceprevention/datasources/index.html
- National Take Back the Night Foundation: https://takebackthenight.org/

**O Beloved Parent**

And companion to us all
Light of day and Dark of night
Earth and sky, Land and sea
Heart of the Seasons:
Light of our hearts
Bring to us these four gifts
Upon the winds
Blow upon us the
Breezes of patience, that
We may learn the value of time
Kiss us with the
Wind of honesty, that we
May understand the heart of Truth
Fill us with the
Breath of faithfulness, that we
May remain steady in Love
Touch us with the air of
Forgiveness, that we may
Know the gift of being forgiven

Thank You, O Beloved of Life,
For these blessed gifts bestowed.

Amen

*Revised 2023*

# Acknowledgments

~~~

## 2023

I am thankful for the many blessings that have come my way since the days when I was the girl in the shadows. Finding my daughter and learning that she was raised by loving parents, along with two brothers who, like her, were adopted. I thank the parents who raised her into the creative, happy, and loving woman she has become.

## *From the 2017 Edition:*

I have been reminded recently that I owe a great thanks to my friend Debbie Kennedy, my poetry sister and first publishing partner in our endeavor *Gypsy Press*; and to Zsuzsanna Budapest, founder of Susan B. Anthony Coven and president of the Women's Spirituality Forum, for their encouragement and inspiration in the very early days as I pounded out the beginning of this book on my old portable typewriter. One more: my friend Anjanette Bailey, whose eagle eyes caught new typos and whose warrior heart encourages mine!

## Thanks

To the wonderful people who read this book as it became more than an exercise in catharsis: Georgia Kirkpatrick, Rosemary Anderson, and Billie Fidlin. I particularly give kudos to Georgia Kirkpatrick for her diligent professional proofreading skills, as well as her "listening ear."

To my family for the love and support as I enter a new and exciting phase of my life.

Finally, I give thanks to the Divine Something for the strength to survive, the will to grow, and the capacity to learn and to move on.

# Index of Chapters and Poetry

Preface to the Anniversary Edition ............................................. 1
Prologue: The Little Girl ............................................................ 3
    The Fire ..................................................................................... 3
      Growing Up ............................................................................ 6
      Phoenix .................................................................................... 9
Interim 1: The Girl in the Corner .............................................. 11
Chapter 1: The Price of Innocence ............................................ 15
    Clean Heart .............................................................................. 16
Chapter 2: Into Darkness ............................................................ 18
    Submission vs. Dominance ..................................................... 21
    Identity Crisis .......................................................................... 22
Chapter 3: The Princess .............................................................. 25
    Sanctuary? ............................................................................... 29
    Birthdays in January ............................................................... 30
    Eleven ...................................................................................... 31
Chapter 4: The Fragility of Friendship ..................................... 32
    Brand ....................................................................................... 36
    October's Cold, Hard Pavements ........................................... 38
Chapter 5: The Risk of Reverie .................................................. 40
    Methinks .................................................................................. 41
    Chamber Music ....................................................................... 42
    A Band of Gold ....................................................................... 45
Chapter 6: Driving for Dummies ............................................... 46
    The Willow .............................................................................. 48
Chapter 7: Imagination and Education ..................................... 50
    Agatha Reborn ........................................................................ 51
    Glaciers .................................................................................... 56
    Catharine's Dark Night .......................................................... 59
    Rappelling ............................................................................... 61
Chapter 8: The Eye of the Beholder .......................................... 63
    Woman of Principle ............................................................... 66

| | |
|---|---|
| Pebbles | 67 |
| **Chapter 9: The Ties Unbound** | **68** |
|    The Origins of Peace | 68 |
|    Salt of My Tears | 71 |
|    Socorro by Midnight | 74 |
| **Interim 2: Back in the Mirror** | **76** |
| **Chapter 10: Blood-Rites** | **77** |
|    Rocking Horse | 78 |
|    Rockers | 86 |
|    K 16 | 91 |
|    The Sale | 93 |
|    K – Epilogue One | 96 |
|    To The Guitarist | 97 |
|    I have found | 97 |
|    I have a soul; it raises up | 97 |
|    Each time you stroke | 97 |
|    Your guitar and I | 97 |
|    Am moved – with shivers | 97 |
|    Running; tingling in time | 97 |
|    With your ever gentle touch | 97 |
|    Along my neck --- | 97 |
|    Your neck – | 97 |
|    The neck of your guitar | 97 |
|    Each deep-bent string of steel | 97 |
|    Becomes my heart, and I | 97 |
|    Can feel the soaring | 97 |
|    Of the ecstasy you play | 97 |
|    In me | 97 |
|    It stays in me | 97 |
|    A sleeping dream, | 97 |
|    Awakened by the astral touch | 97 |

Your music has ......... 97
Upon my mind ......... 97

## Chapter 11: Phoenix and the Rock Star ......... 98
ChristSonnet ......... 101

## Chapter 12: Rock-n-Roll Reality ......... 102
Angelic ......... 107

Soul-Mate ......... 110

## Chapter 13: The Girl in the Song ......... 111
Artist ......... 112

The Girl in the Song ......... 118

## Chapter 14: Elf-Witch ......... 120
ElfWitch's Wishsong ......... 120

The Speech ......... 121

Lost Soul ......... 125

*Soul Food* ......... 129

## Interim 3: Through the Glass, Darkly ......... 130
Woman ......... 131

## Chapter 15: Beachmare ......... 132
Dark Dungeon ......... 137

Broken Promises ......... 138

Space-Time ......... 139

## Interim 4: The Scrying Mirror ......... 140
Chamomile Dreams ......... 141

## Chapter 16: From the Ashes… ......... 142
Sweet, He Left ......... 144

3 a.m. ......... 146

Holy Ground ......... 148

Labor ......... 152

## Interim 5: Dark Moon ......... 153
## Chapter 17: Forgiveness ......... 154
New In You ......... 156

## Chapter 18: New Life ......... 157
Drawing Down the Moon ......... 159

    The Forest .................................................................................... 161

    Lord, Lord ................................................................................... 164

    Regret .......................................................................................... 166

    I; Dorcas ..................................................................................... 168

Interim 6: A New Kind of Glass ................................................ 171

Chapter 19: Reunion .................................................................. 173

    L(ove) .......................................................................................... 175

    Y(outh) ....................................................................................... 176

Statistics* .................................................................................... 178

Resources ................................................................................... 179

    O Beloved Parent ...................................................................... 180

    **Index of Chapters and Poetry ............................................... 185**

Made in the USA
Las Vegas, NV
03 September 2023

77011960R00121